# THIS IS
# PLAY

## Environments and Interactions that Engage Infants and Toddlers

Julia Luckenbill, Aarti Subramaniam, & Janet Thompson

National Association for the Education of Young Children
Washington, DC

# naeyc®

National Association for the Education of Young Children
1313 L Street NW, Suite 500
Washington, DC 20005-4101
202-232-8777 • 800-424-2460
NAEYC.org

## NAEYC Books

Senior Director, Publishing and Professional Learning
*Susan Friedman*

Former Editor in Chief
*Kathy Charner*

Senior Editor
*Holly Bohart*

Editor
*Rossella Procopio*

Senior Creative Design Manager
*Henrique J. Siblesz*

Senior Creative Design Specialist
*Gillian Frank*

Publishing Business Operations Manager
*Francine Markowitz*

Through its publications program, the National Association for the Education of Young Children (NAEYC) provides a forum for discussion of major issues and ideas in the early childhood field, with the hope of provoking thought and promoting professional growth. The views expressed or implied in this book are not necessarily those of the Association.

**Permissions**

NAEYC accepts requests for limited use of our copyrighted material. For permission to reprint, adapt, translate, or otherwise reuse and repurpose content from this publication, review our guidelines at NAEYC.org/resources/permissions.

**Photo Credits**

Copyright © NAEYC: 19, 20, 28, 65, and 117

Copyright © Getty Images: cover, vi, 4, 24, 26, 27, 32, 39, 43, 48, 52, 57, 61, 70, 75, 86, 89, 90, 94, 114, and 128

Courtesy of Julia Luckenbill: v, 3, 14, 44, 46, 59, 68, 78, 93, 96, 98, 105, 108, 110, and 122

**This Is Play: Environments and Interactions that Engage Infants and Toddlers.** Copyright © 2019 by the National Association for the Education of Young Children. All rights reserved. Printed in the United States of America.

Library of Congress Control Number: 2019935619

ISBN: 978-1-938113-53-6

Item 1141

# Contents

**1**   **Introduction**

     2      Developmentally Appropriate Practice

**5**   **Chapter 1:** The Importance of Play for Young Children

     8      What Is Play and What Does It Mean for Infants and Toddlers?

     12      Why Do Adults Need to Facilitate Infants' and Toddlers' Play?

     13      What Does It Mean to Facilitate Young Children's Play?

     21      Connect and Communicate with Families

     22      Document Children's Play and Learning

     23      Where to Find More: Resources for Teachers and Famillies

**25**   **Chapter 2:** The Young Infant: Birth to 9 Months

     26      What's an Infant Like from Birth to 3 Months?

     27      What's an Infant Like at 3 to 6 Months?

     28      What's an Infant Like at 6 to 9 Months?

     29      What's a Teacher of Young Infants Like?

     29      The Teacher's Role: Be Caring and Responsive

     38      An Engaging Environment for Young Infants: Simple and Soothing

     47      Where to Find More: Resources for Teachers and Families

**49**    **Chapter 3:** The Mobile Infant: 8 to 18 Months

     50      What's an Infant Like at 8 to 12 Months?

     51      What's an Infant Like at 12 to 18 Months?

     52      What's a Teacher of Mobile Infants Like?

     53      The Teacher's Role: Provide a Safe Environment for Exploring

     62      An Engaging Environment for Mobile Infants: Safe and Inviting for Exploration

     69      Where to Find More: Resources for Teachers and Families

**71**    **Chapter 4:** The Toddler: 16 to 36 Months

     72      What's a Toddler Like at 16 to 24 Months?

     73      What's a Toddler Like at 24 to 30 Months?

     74      What's a Toddler Like at 30 to 36 Months?

     75      What's a Teacher of Toddlers Like?

     76      The Teacher's Role: Engage Children in New Experiences and Help Them Navigate Interactions

     92      An Engaging Environment for Toddlers: More Complex Opportunities for Investigating and Interacting

     113      Where to Find More: Resources for Teachers and Families

**115**    **Chapter 5:** Working with Children with Diverse Characteristics, Abilities, and Needs

     116      Partner with Families Using a Strengths-Based Model

     117      Strategies for Supporting Children in Play

     121      Where to Find More: Resources for Teachers and Families

**123**    **Conclusion**

**123**    **Acknowledgments**

**124**    **References**

**127**    **About the Authors**

# Introduction

Play is often talked about as if it were a relief from serious learning. But for children, play is serious learning.

—Fred Rogers, quoted in "Why Play Is the Work of Childhood"

Children's experiences in the first three years of life lay the foundation for strong relationships, fruitful learning, and healthy social and emotional skills. From birth, infants are actively engaged in making sense of all that surrounds them. They observe, then experiment with whatever catches their attention, testing their ability to figure things out and make something happen. They interact with the people in their world, driven to engage and encouraged by responsive partners. As their skills and understanding steadily grow during the infant and toddler years, they venture further from their trusted teachers to explore their interests. Their confidence grows.

Children accomplish all of this when they play. Play motivates them to build and test their growing competence—in engaging positively with people, mastering physical and intellectual tasks, and acting out the stories created by their imaginations. In play, they choose their own pursuits and direct their own learning.

As a teacher for very young children, you have a significant role: you facilitate the play that nurtures their growth in all areas of development and builds on each child's interests, abilities, and developmental progress. To effectively take on this task, you begin with a deep knowledge of early development. With that foundation, you can observe and document the development of each child in your care. That ongoing documentation guides you in developing a truly individualized curriculum centered on play and exploration along with care routines.

For example, really knowing and understanding each infant and toddler will help you

> Decide how to interact with each infant in personalized ways
> Design your setting—indoors and outdoors—with furnishings, equipment, and materials that will stimulate children's desire to play in creative ways and build new skills and understandings

Young children depend on the consistent support you provide for the play that is their work. In an infant or toddler classroom, facilitating play should be taken as seriously as ensuring children's safety and attending to care routines. When you value and support their play, children thrive—both as individuals and as a classroom community.

## Terms Used in this Book

If you are engaged in caring for infants or toddlers, you may describe yourself as a *caregiver*. Your day is filled with care routines and each child develops a secure, trusting relationship with you because you provide the care she needs.

In this book, we have chosen to use *teacher* to describe your role in the infant and toddler care setting. You are an early childhood educator, just as teachers of preschool-age children and primary students are, and the title of *teacher* acknowledges the specialized skills, knowledge, and training that make all

of you members of the same profession. You engage in responsive, playful interactions with each child that are informed by your knowledge of their developmental pathways and your ability to support their growth.

The word *classroom* is used to refer to any space where infants, toddlers, and teachers together explore, learn, and stretch themselves, whether it be a center, school, family child care home, or other setting.

# Developmentally Appropriate Practice

Your decisions about *how* to nurture children's play and learning—and partnering with families in those decisions—can be guided by what's known from research about how children develop and the care and education practices that are considered effective. Your knowledge, experience, and relationships with the children will guide you to provide just enough novelty and just enough challenge to stimulate but not overwhelm them.

Through play, you can provide a bridge from where children are and what they can do to a place of new knowledge and understanding. This requires several considerations: understanding children's overall development; understanding the ways individual children approach learning; establishing realistic learning objectives; and matching strategies to each child's culture and current interests, knowledge, and skills.

As you provide experiences and choose strategies to support children in their play, remember to consider the following (NAEYC 2009):

> Begin with a solid grounding in child development, aware of what children are generally able to do and interested in at the ages represented in your classroom. This helps you know what experiences and interactions are likely to be appropriate for infants and toddlers and to set realistic goals for them.

> Consider each child's interests and abilities (everyone learns best when invited to choose their own learning opportunities). Keep in mind that children vary: each develops at a unique pace, displaying both strengths and areas that need more support. This means, for example, that if you have an infant who cannot

yet reach learning materials on a table, you might place some of the materials at a lower location she can reach, but you also offer specific opportunities and support to encourage the child to pull herself to a standing position.

> Provide materials and experiences that respect and represent the cultures and family structures of the children you work with. This begins as you design your room before the children even join you and evolves as the children grow and as new families join your program.

---

This book will guide you to play and interact with infants and toddlers in ways that respect their individual development and family cultures, are responsive to their cues, and promote their optimal learning. Chapters 2–4 explore what infants and toddlers are like and environments and experiences that support and enhance their development, beginning with young infants, then looking at mobile infants, and finally examining toddlers. Each chapter includes

> A snapshot of a child's development and play at that age
> Suggestions for supporting children's development through play
> Practical ideas for the classroom environment and materials
> Suggested resources for teachers and families

Observing children, responding to their cues, providing a supportive environment, and enthusiastically entering into their play—these are the foundations for a trusting relationship that infants and toddlers can use as a launching pad to explore their world!

# 1

# The Importance of Play for Young Children

When we appreciate the important role play serves in a child's learning about self and world, we give children the time and opportunity to engage in the self-initiated play that is the surest way for them to fully realize all of their intellectual, emotional, and social potential.

—David Elkind, *The Wisdom of Play: How Children Learn to Make Sense of the World*

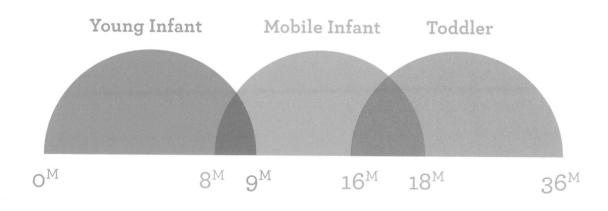

Young Infant    Mobile Infant    Toddler

0ᴹ        8ᴹ  9ᴹ      16ᴹ  18ᴹ        36ᴹ

While infant and toddler play may not look like the play of older children, this is where play begins. The foundations of play are in the early relationships that a newborn forms with the people and the world around her. For example, the responses she receives from her first social smiles support later, more complex interactions with you and with others in her world. These interactions, which are the beginning of play behavior, may be harder to recognize as play than the more typical activity of preschoolers.

When a very young child is playing, it may look random, unstructured, or like nothing much is happening. For example, a toddler walking on a wet street may stomp in each puddle, staring at the splashes that result and then stomping some more. When you observe closely, you see that this child is busy at play—and learning. He is experimenting with cause and effect (I can make the water splash with my feet!), making comparisons (stomp harder, make bigger splashes), and noticing different sensations on his skin (dry vs. wet). Through play like this, young children are actually learning basic principles of science and math (Cohen & Emmons 2017).

Here are some more examples of what play looks like at very young ages:

## Play at 6, 15, 24, and 30 months

Tomas (6 months) is on his tummy, a basket of wooden and plastic rattles in front of him. His eyes and mouth are both open wide. He squeals, then reaches out and grasps a bright orange ridged rattle. He brings it to his mouth, turning his wrist and mouthing the surface until the handle reaches his lips. He rubs the handle against his mouth, then drops the rattle. He reaches out to repeat the process with a second rattle, a wooden one. Each rattle has a unique color and texture, and Tomas is beginning to learn about these characteristics as he mouths them. Although this exploration is slow and the learning is subtle, Tomas's teacher lets him mouth several different ones and does not interrupt his play or try to show him something new by shaking the rattles. She talks to him about the different textures he's experiencing.

Jurnee (15 months) is exploring a three-piece puzzle. She lifts two pieces, but rather than put them back in their holes, she bangs them together like a pair of cymbals. Then she tries to fit one into her mouth. No luck. She abandons the pieces and toddles away. Although Jurnee's teacher might choose another moment to coach Jurnee to put the pieces in the holes, in this moment he realizes that Jurnee is learning about the puzzle pieces in her own way and that this gathering of knowledge is valid too.

East (24 months) is cradling a plastic baby doll in his arms. He rocks it back and forth, then places it on the couch. Walking to the corner of the house area, he picks up a blanket, carries it back to the doll, and gently covers the doll, leaving the face showing. He kisses the face, then turns to reach for a small clipboard and pencil.

East is showing his teacher that he has observed and can imitate the care he sees given to his small cousin at home. His teacher, knowing that having a new baby in the family is a significant life change for little ones, has provided East with both the space for "talking about" his life through play and the props to do so.

At a family child care center, children are watching a show outdoors about bees. Sarah (30 months) is focused on the piles of oak pollen and dust on the ground. She looks over and sees an older child drawing in the dust with a stick and imitates him, using a small stick to trace ovals in the dust. Next she makes piles of twigs. She notices tiny acorns in the piles and extends them to her teacher, asking if something so small can be an acorn.

Sarah's teacher does not try to refocus her attention on the bee show that the older children are enjoying. She knows that Sarah is learning about the properties of the dust, refining her motor skills as she writes and picks up items, learning math as she sorts and labels the acorns and reflects on their size, and engaging in parallel play (imitating and playing with materials in a similar way as another child nearby but not influencing or being influenced by the other child).

All these children are learning in the way young children learn best: not through adult direction or being coached to use a material in a certain way, but by making their own choices from carefully selected toys and materials and exploring them under the watchful eye of an adult who knows them well. The children are eagerly researching the world and how it works, in their own ways. Their teachers are aware of the children's interests and capabilities, the learning that may be occurring through play, and when it's best to step in or just observe.

## This book uses the following general age ranges for infants and toddlers:

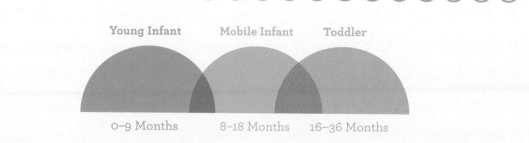

| Young Infant | Mobile Infant | Toddler |
| --- | --- | --- |
| 0–9 Months | 8–18 Months | 16–36 Months |

Adapted from "DAP with Infants and Toddlers, Ages Birth–3," NAEYC. NAEYC.org/resources/topics/dap/infants-and-toddlers.

# What Is Play and What Does It Mean for Infants and Toddlers?

Like play itself, the many definitions of play are varied. Psychologist Peter Gray (2008) notes several widely recognized characteristics of play:

> Play is something chosen by the players, an activity they engage in just for its own sake.

> The players determine the content of the play, including the structure and rules.

> Players are free to stop anytime, and they're engaged in the activity but are not stressed by it.

> Because play is shaped by the imagination, it follows different rules than those found in real life.

Through play, children learn to persist, interact, engage, invent, and act out their ideas and share them. Play affirms and stimulates children's creativity and nurtures the "thinking outside the box" approach that children will use to contribute their own ideas to the world. As Piaget notes, "Play is the answer to the question: how does anything new come about?" (quoted in Elkind 2008, 3).

As children engage in self-led, open-ended play with you and by themselves, they are building the foundations of later learning (Petersen 2012). They are also gaining social skills (Ramani 2012) and learning to work well with others—important for the classroom, home, and eventual school success.

## Types of Play

Understanding some of the different ways that very young children play can help you support them where they're at and gently introduce more complex interactions and exploration. Here are some common types of play you'll see infants and toddlers engaging in (Kid Sense, n.d.; White, n.d.; Yogman et al. 2018).

**Interpersonal play.** Social and emotional exchanges between infants and peers or teachers are a basic form of play. Through play with others, infants use teachers as secure bases for exploring their environment. These interactions help infants develop a sense of self. Examples: peekaboo and cooing back and forth.

**Exploratory or sensorimotor play.** Children explore objects to understand what they are and what can be done with them. Examples: banging, mouthing, shaking, or handling and throwing objects or materials.

# Play Is Essential to Children's Development

Long before they develop the ability to use language to ask questions about the world around them, young children investigate it using their senses. They look, hear, taste, smell, touch, and move, exploring and discovering at their own pace to expand what they know and understand.

**Gaining skills and knowledge.** Play supports children's skills across all developmental domains: social and emotional, language (Ramani 2012), cognitive, self-help, and large and small motor (Bongiorno 2019). By actively exploring objects and people, infants and toddlers discover things like the following (Piaget, quoted in Maguire-Fong 2015):

> The properties or characteristics of objects, such as soft, heavy, slippery, cold
> The relationship between objects, such as size, order, number, and pattern; cause and effect; and the experience of time
> The language and behaviors we use to communicate with and understand each other and the world

Play is the vehicle for helping children make progress toward the learning goals you have for them. It builds skills they'll use throughout their lives, such as solving problems, interacting and negotiating with others, processing emotions, taking risks, flexibility, resilience, and self-direction (Pathways.org 2019).

**A way to practice.** Play is also a way for children to prepare for adult tasks. When a toddler imitates your diapering routines, his play may look routine and unimportant. But it allows him to accomplish a couple of things: master the world he inhabits now and build the confidence and skills he will need to approach new challenges as he encounters them.

**Relational play.** Children explore how objects can be combined in play, often imitating the use of objects they have observed. Examples: using a pitcher to pour juice or a spoon to stir in a cup.

**Constructive play.** Children use open-ended materials—blocks, sand, paint—to create something. They are able to think about something before they try to construct it. Examples: stacking several blocks or problem solving how to extract a stuck ball from a tube.

**Symbolic play.** Also known as dramatic or pretend play, this type of play involves using one object as another object, idea, or action. Older toddlers may act out simple story lines that involve several players. Example: using sand as food in a pretend kitchen, taking on roles in the kitchen.

**Rough-and-tumble play.** This form of play occurs at all ages and is characterized by engaging in playful physical actions. Examples: crawling over other infants, pulling opposite each other on a length of fabric.

**Regulating emotions and actions.** Right along with learning how to move and talk and make things happen, infants and toddlers are gradually learning to focus their attention, control their impulses, make decisions, manage strong feelings, resist their urges to push or grab to get what they want right now, and negotiate play rules. Play is an excellent way for them to practice these complex self-regulation skills because the pleasure of playing with others motivates children to develop them (Galinsky 2010). For example, while playing, toddlers gradually learn—with lots of support from you!—ways to resolve conflicts over toys or play plans in ways that work for all the players.

## Electronic Toys and Screen Devices

Many toys for very young children feature flashing lights, noises, and music. Be aware that these toys can be overstimulating for very young children and can contribute to making the classroom loud and chaotic.

Videos and cell phone apps are sometimes marketed as tools that make babies smarter. However, having face-to-face interactions with infants and toddlers makes you a far more effective play and learning partner than screens or devices. When you speak, sing, and smile in response to a child, you're showing her how relationships work—something she doesn't learn from a toy or screen. These interactions allow children to try out and refine their communication and language skills and to receive a smile that says that they are valued and loved and that their ideas are exciting and worth exploring. Throughout this book you'll find suggestions for materials and activities that are more appropriate choices for supporting the development of infants and toddlers than most electronic toys and devices.

# Play Helps Children Handle Stress and Conflict

When challenges or stresses arise during play—a ball won't fit into a hole, there aren't enough shovels for all the players, the "blanket" a child made from a leaf tore apart— children gradually learn to handle the stressful, unpleasant, or challenging situations and to solve the problem rather than respond with an outburst of emotion or simply stop playing. Through play, children learn how to approach challenges in a constructive way, as Ansel and Frida are doing:

### Smoothing over a spoon dispute with a 26- and 27-month-old

Ansel (27 months) and Frida (26 months) are standing in front of a plastic baby doll in the sand kitchen, a pretend kitchen with real running water for symbolic play. "Dere's two spoons—one for you and one for me," Ansel says as he places two small plastic spoons in a bowl and walks to the stack of plates. Frida takes both small spoons, using them like salad tongs to scoop up sand and put it in a bowl. Their teacher comments,

"Oh, Ansel is setting the table and you are making the food, Frida." "It's pasta!" trumpets Frida. "It's tasty!" "And Ansel is getting a serving spoon. It's big," comments the teacher as Ansel picks up a large spoon.

She continues to narrate: "Frida is serving with two spoons." Ansel looks over at the bowl and sees that both spoons are gone. He frowns and looks at Frida. "But I need a small spoon too," he says loudly. Frida grins and hands him a spoon, and they both smile. Together they serve the sand pasta onto the plates.

In his role as the server, Ansel demonstrates more patience with the plan change around the spoons than his teacher has seen him do in other situations. He is able to relax into the game and serve the food rather than remain irritated that Frida has ignored his initial cue about sharing the spoons ("one for you and one for me"). The skillful narration of their teacher helps both children see each other's play bids—their attempts to engage each other and share their own points of view—and keeps the game running smoothly.

## Play Helps Children Focus

As children play, they develop the ability to concentrate for longer and longer periods of time (Wang & Barrett 2013). A very young infant may focus just a moment or two on your playful face. An older infant may be able to focus long enough to track several balls as they travel down a ball drop and under a shelf, and a toddler may be able to complete a nine-piece knob puzzle. This active, focused engagement with a challenging task—often called a *state of flow* (Csikszentmihalyi 2014)—is something children learn to cultivate through their play. It will continue to be important as they enter more complex and challenging learning environments. You encourage children to persist in trying things when you make comments and suggestions as they play, expand on their language or actions, and change up an activity or make it a little more complex.

> **Miles at 30 Months**
>
> Mom: What is play?
> Miles: Ummm, Mommy?
> Mom: How do you know if you're playing?
> Miles: My friends are there.

## Play Supports Creativity

Children develop creative thinking skills when they explore and problem solve during play. For example, when young children are shown how a toy works, they often use the toy only in the way it was demonstrated and then discard it. But when children are asked to find out for themselves how a toy works, they focus on the task longer and discover new or more effective ways to use it (Bonawitz et al. 2011). While it's important for you to interact with children as they play and to respond to their cues, they will learn more and be more engaged if you direct their play less and look for ways to support their own ideas. Chapters 2–4 offer many practical strategies for doing this.

As children engage in play experiences with others, they begin to be able to resist the impulse to take play materials—and hang on to them so no one else can get them! Instead, they learn to consider alternatives that might be more creative or innovative or reflect the needs and interests of other children. This process takes many years, but through social play, young children build the confidence to figure things out and trust their own creative solutions to life's challenges (Berk & Meyers 2013).

# Why Do Adults Need to Facilitate Infants' and Toddlers' Play?

Children will learn through play even if they do not experience the kind of mindful teacher support described throughout this book. Why, then, does it matter what a teacher does with infants and toddlers as they play?

## You Expand Learning Opportunities

If you provide well-timed, tuned-in feedback and gentle task support, you can *scaffold* a child's learning—guide her to learn and accomplish something she can't do by herself right now. By describing the ongoing action, asking open-ended questions, coaching interactions, and providing materials when a child needs them, you expand the learning possibilities of any play scenario.

Tuning in to a child's needs and ideas and joining her as she explores materials allows you to

> Expand the child's vocabulary by labeling her actions and toys during play
> Support her social skills by inviting her to take turns with you and with peers and working through disputes
> Expand the play and encourage more complex thinking by giving her hints for a new play idea or technique or by making connections to things in her life
> Promote persistence by guiding the child to a solution when things get hard—expressing how hard or frustrating it is when tasks go awry and then gently helping her refocus on the task

### Scaffolding with an 18- and 19-month-old

Teacher Nathan is seated with Miriam (18 months). From a basket of brightly colored teething necklaces, Miriam chooses one. She presses it to her head, then frowns. Nathan comments, "It looks like you want to put that necklace on over your head. You look frustrated. That looks hard." Miriam looks at him. "Your mama was wearing a necklace," Nathan continues. "I wonder if she opened it up before she put it over her head. Maybe she used both hands?" Miriam hands him the necklace. He opens it with both hands and puts it over his head, then hands her a second necklace. With a wrinkled forehead, Miriam grasps the necklace and opens it as Nathan has modeled, then places it over her own head. She grins. "You did it!" Nathan cheers. "Now we are both wearing necklaces!" Kaleo (19 months) walks over, his eyes on Miriam's necklace. "Hi, Kaleo," Nathan says. "Miriam and I are wearing necklaces! Want to use mine?" He takes his off, modeling taking turns with materials, and Kaleo grins and takes it.

## You Help Children Recognize and Handle Their Emotions

As you observe the challenges children have as they play, offer comments about what you see and hear and help them find some satisfying resolutions. By doing this, you enable children to process and handle their emotions. When you observe a toddler repeatedly diapering a doll, for example, you can affirm how hard it is to have a new baby sibling and how the toddler is such a good big brother.

When you hear a toddler demand that the doll stay in one bed while he is in another bed, you can comment that the doll must have a new big kid bed now. This creates space for the child to express his feelings to a supportive person—you.

# What Does It Mean to Facilitate Young Children's Play?

For infants and toddlers to fully experience the benefits of play and interaction with others, they depend on you to do several things: provide a sense of safety and security, offer just the right kind and amount of stimulation and support at the right times, be relaxed and playful, and meet their individual needs.

## Provide a Secure Base

Infant and toddler play happens in the context of a *secure base*—a person the child trusts and can turn to when he's anxious or upset. A secure base acts as both a safe place for a child to *be* and a place for her to recharge before she goes back out to explore the world.

### Exploring and recharging at 8 and 26 months

James (8 months) is lying on the grass beside his teacher. He caresses the grass and pinches small sticks, lifting them to his face. His teacher comments, "You're touching the grass. It's soft." Although his teacher does not appear to be doing much as she sits beside James and narrates, she is essential to his play. Her presence and calm voice make him feel secure enough to explore.

Aliah (26 months) loves to run across the grass and onto the climber. She mounts the stairs, then looks out to her teacher with a grin, checking that someone has seen her climb. After she slides down the slide, she runs back to her teacher, who gives her a big hug and comments on her accomplishment. Aliah runs off to try it again. This too is secure base behavior—when a toddler explores a new space, she needs to be able to return to a trusted teacher for a recharge.

Exploring the child care setting is a brave act for an infant or toddler. He leaves a familiar home and his family to come to an unfamiliar place—and then his family leaves him! Many infants and toddlers protest this separation by crying or withdrawing. It is essential for you to build connections with children and families by being predictable, supportive, and responsive to these feelings.

An infant or toddler will explore and learn *if* she feels that she is safe and that her needs will be met (Erikson 1950) and after she has come to terms with separation and understands that her family will return each time. You help provide that sense of safety and trust by being sensitive and responsive to a child's cues and the family's actions and emotions.

# Apply Your Understanding of How Children Develop

Being aware of infant and toddler development in general and of children's individual development guides your curriculum planning, the way you design your setting, and how you provide individual learning experiences for each child. It also makes you more aware of possible developmental delays, allowing you to design experiences that support children's needs and expand their learning through play.

**Start with where children are and gradually add complexity.** Knowing what a child can do and what she might be ready for next can help you determine where to begin with an infant or toddler in the social–emotional "dance" that is your relationship with her. This knowledge also helps you understand what you can do to support and expand her skills through playful interactions.

For example, you know that infants and toddlers take in many sights, sounds, smells, tastes, and textures as they interact with the environment, and that they use this sensory information to try out ideas, act on them, change them, and try out their new ideas. So, you can provide opportunities for children to engage with a rich variety of objects and invite them into social interactions.

Offer very young infants a range of objects that are safe to handle, mouth, bang, and throw. Respond to their cries and coos, which provides a model for them for how to respond to another person's intent to communicate. As they get older, plan learning opportunities that are more complex to match their increasing ability to use tools and other objects more intentionally, solve basic problems, and interact in more complex ways.

In a room with young infants, for example, you might offer baskets of balls of different textures for children to explore. When the infants are older, provide a drop box with two holes at the top. Most balls will fit and will fall vertically to the base of the toy to be reclaimed.

Once children have mastered this activity, provide a marble-drop style toy that invites them to track balls on diagonal paths and can even be taken apart and redesigned. Each toy builds on the key concepts from the previous activity and adds complexity based on children's emerging developmental skills and the ways they explore toys.

**Be open to the novel ways children explore.** Adults often attend to the things they do with a spotlight-like focus. Infants and toddlers, however, experience things in a more lantern-like way, their focus extending in all directions and taking in many things at once (Gopnik 2009). When you put out toys and plan activities for children, targeting particular interests and developmental needs, you may intend for children to use the materials in a certain way. But working with infants and toddlers requires you to be open to a wide range of ways they can use and learn about the toys, and all are valuable. Children's thinking and play can teach you a great deal about yourself and your willingness to adapt.

## Create and Maintain an Intentional Environment

The classroom (and outdoor) environment and the materials in it provide a backdrop and inspiration for children's learning. When you place things in the space and invite the children to use them, you must do so thoughtfully. The space itself should be inviting but not overwhelming.

Look around your space. How do children respond to what's there? If there are too many items in the room, children may become overstimulated and unable to focus. Having too few items available or materials that rarely get changed out often leads to conflicts over toys or boredom with the choices. Items that lend themselves only to basic discoveries that children have already made don't challenge them, and this too can lead to conflict or boredom. Too much visual clutter distracts children; and walls that are too sterile provide an institutional look rather than a welcoming, homelike setting.

To balance children's need for stimulation with their need for calm, carefully create "a calm environment with a focus on learning that accommodates the children's development. Materials should be open ended but not overwhelming. The space may differ, but these things are universal" (Peter Mangione, personal communication, July 21, 2015).

Plan each part of the room with care so that it invites a certain number of learners (for example, place two toy pianos side by side) and lets adults gently guide the play (for example, with enough space for you to sit beside the two piano players). Include areas with soft, inviting features where children can take a break as well as areas where they can move and explore. Select items that reflect the homes and cultures of the children in your class as well as individual interests. Chapters 2–4 offer more detailed suggestions for creating inviting learning environments for infants and toddlers.

## Use Responsive Play Strategies

The most important strategy for supporting and enriching children's play is to read their cues and respond in sensitive ways. Caring for infants and toddlers and supporting their development requires you to understand their very different ways of thinking and playing and to adapt to their needs.

At times you will need to slow down, speed up, or pull back from an interaction. While *you* might quickly become bored with something as simple as a fallen leaf, an infant can be entranced with smashing it, tossing it, or striking the grass with it. Because play is the tool young children use to explore the world, you must engage in their play too, but in *their* ways, respecting their interests and abilities.

Children's exploration and learning don't always happen on adults' timetables. With infants and toddlers, you're often faced with choices about whether to follow along with something a child is interested in at the moment or stick to your schedule or plan. In these cases, think about the learning that might occur if you set aside *your* plans and follow the child's.

In the following two vignettes, an infant discovers some green paint just before snack time. In each, the teacher responds differently.

### A teacher, an infant, and green paint 1

An older infant crawls over to the sensory table, pulls to stand, and smears the paint. It has mostly dried, but a bit gets on her hands. Her eyes widen. She stares at the paint, then her hands. She eases back to the floor and crawls away, tracking small green handprints. The teacher sighs and cleans up the paint and the green prints.

### A teacher, an infant, and green paint 2

You were planning to clean up the table for snack in about five minutes, but you notice an older infant has crawled over and is patting the dry green paint on the paper. You walk over, kneel, and put a bit more wet green paint out on the paper as you narrate your actions: "I'm squeezing some paint on the paper. It's okay to paint." The infant then smears some of the paint on her hands. Wearing a wide smile, you exclaim, "You have green hands!" The infant stares at her painted skin and then proceeds to smear the green on the paper. "And now there is green on the paper too!" you say.

The first scenario resulted in some missed opportunities to extend the infant's learning. In the second scenario, the infant had opportunities to focus on the concept of color, develop her motor skills, explore cause and effect, expand her language, use her hands as tools to paint, and cope with an interesting sensory experience. All this was gained through a simple social interaction with the adult, centered around play rather than a rush to clean up and be efficient.

Although there certainly are adult tasks to be done in a timely manner in every infant or toddler room, following a child's lead is a gift you can choose to give.

**Play *with* children.** Join children in their play activity, at their level on the floor or at a table. Stay long enough so that the child feels that you have noticed what he is doing and that his ideas are worth observing. Be aware, however, of those times when you might be caught up in a beautiful play interaction with a child and so tuned in to him that you lose track of the rest of the classroom and the other children's needs.

**Empower children to try things on their own.** Allow a child to freely explore when she seeks it and provide opportunities to participate in her own care. As children play and perhaps struggle with a task, first be silent and observe. Then you can decide how to provide support in a way that does not take over children's ideas but builds on them.

There is an art to making gentle suggestions rather than simply solving a problem quickly for a child. One way is to use "I wonder" statements. For example, saying, "I wonder if the pizza cutter rolls too, like the rolling pin" may be just enough support for him to try a different solution himself rather than use you as a tool to get the task done. Then you can ease out of the situation and let the child continue the play, perhaps just checking in with him occasionally. If you can encourage the child's focus and persistence in a way in which he does most of the work, he'll be more likely to own the solution and use it again in another situation.

**Scaffold children's play and learning.** When you create a bridge that connects what a child already knows and can do with new knowledge and understanding, you are scaffolding his play (Gillespie & Greenberg 2017). As a result, the child accomplishes or moves toward a skill or concept he may not be able to do or understand on his own yet. For example, you might change a child's game with you slightly to see if it holds his attention a little longer and encourages him to try a new strategy. Or maybe you offer a little hint when a child is having difficulty fitting in a puzzle piece just the right way. Gradually, you withdraw your support until the child is able to do the skill on his own. This book discusses many strategies for scaffolding children's play and learning.

**Narrate children's play.** Narrating what a child is doing is also an effective way to support and scaffold her play. This technique is sometimes called *sportscasting* because you talk aloud as a sportscaster does—telling about the plotline of the game, including actions, perspectives, and possible next moves. You can also say what *you* are doing.

How do you decide what to say? Here are some possibilities:

> Use **parallel talk**, commenting on what the child is doing: "You have a big red ball!"
> Use **reflective speech**, guessing at a child's feelings and motivations: "It looks like you might want to throw it!" "Quinn looks like he wants a ball too."
> **Expand on what the child is saying** by repeating it and then saying a longer sentence that includes what the child said: "Ball? Yes, that's a big red ball!"
> Use **self-talk** to explain what you are doing or what you are going to do and to keep a situation predictable for the child: "I'm going to get you a tissue while you play with the ball, Catalina. I'll be right back."

When you sportscast, be careful to "bathe the child in language" rather than drown her in a verbal flood (Lally et al. 1998). Watch the child's body language for clues for when and how to respond. Is she looking down at what she is doing? Your narration at that point may actually interfere with her play. Is she looking up for feedback from you, making a face that indicates she's frustrated, or smiling at her own success? Narrating in these situations will demonstrate that you are in tune *and* help you support the child's language.

**Keep the individual child in mind.** Adjust your responses to each child based on his unique disposition and culture. If a child is hesitant to explore new experiences, introduce change gradually in an area he does enjoy to encourage him to try something new. For example, if a toddler enjoys using the playdough and rolling pins, keep them available but also add pizza cutters. If a child uses chopsticks at home, having practice chopsticks along with forks in the dramatic play area invites him to develop culturally appropriate self-help skills through play.

Know each child's competencies and individual differences. It's okay to let the infant use you as a tool when she needs some assistance, but invite her to help you. For example, if she is having difficulty pushing hard enough to get a pop-up toy to work, you might say, "Let's do it together, Angeline. Here, press it with me." Then, engage in your own reflection afterward: was the toy perhaps too complex for an infant who does not yet have the strength to work it herself?

Also consider that in some home cultures, it's important for adults to do more for a child than for the child to be able to do something independently. Some families may discourage certain activities. For example, many infants explore their food while also attempting to eat it. If you observe an infant who's not doing anything with her food, it may be because at home she is fed by an adult or because playing with food is not something that is done in her home.

**Adapt your support as children change.** The way you facilitate and enhance play experiences for children will change as they grow older. With a younger child, you might sportscast by using words that simply describe what the child is experiencing. But your questions to an older child could invite him to wonder more about how something works or to try a new way of doing something.

## Let Labels Go

You may wonder how to support play and social interaction for a child with a disability or delay. Linda Brault, director of WestEd's Beginning Together project, suggests that teachers probably already have the tools for including children with disabilities in their programs (personal communication, email, July 5, 2015). If you set aside the label a child may have (or that you think he may have) and consider where he is developmentally, you can simply adapt how you play with him and what materials you present.

For example, a toddler who has Down syndrome may use less language, develop motor skills more slowly, and demonstrate less complex problem solving than other children his age. If you have worked with young infants, you know how to support their emerging walking, talking, and social play skills—it is already in your toolbox. The label *Down syndrome* may make you wonder if you are able to support the child and family, but much of the time, you can successfully include the child if you let the label go and think of him as an individual with unique abilities, interests, and needs.

Linda says this:

> At the Beginning Together Institute, I start off by asking people to imagine that a new 2-year-old is beginning in their classroom the next day. She is really enthusiastic, loves music and singing, can be a bit hard to understand at times, is still a bit wobbly when walking longer distances, and has an incredible smile. Everyone has probably started thinking of things they might do to help her succeed, questions they have for her family, and what they might do to plan for her first day. If I say that she also happens to have Down syndrome, some people will say, "But I don't know how to support a child with Down syndrome," forgetting that the ideas and thoughts they had based on my description of her actual development were a great starting place.

> Experienced infant teachers need to retain what they already know about young children and about making adjustments or adaptations when including a child with a disability or special need. While a child may have a diagnosis or need that impacts his or her development, that child still has many of the same interests, capabilities, and characteristics as other children of a similar age. (personal communication, email, July 5, 2015)

Since each child is unique, you will interact with each child and design experiences for him in ways that are unique. You begin the dance with children at the place where they are. Throughout this book, you'll find examples of ways to be responsive to individual children.

This Is Play

# Connect and Communicate with Families

Children and their families come to your program with their own rich identities, experiences, and backgrounds. Invite families to join in as partners with you, observing how their children grow and thrive through playful interactions both at home and in the program. You will learn much from each other!

**Connect what is happening at home with what is happening in the program.** As you get to know the families, seek ways to honor their practices and preferences. Families are the experts on their children and can provide insights about them that help you individualize the curriculum. Ask them, "Tell me a little more about that" to discover ways to bring some of their home practices into the classroom. Model some basic songs and provide links to them online. In addition, ask families to share songs, chants, and rhymes from their cultures with you. When you give families opportunities to share their home activities, it can enrich the classroom with new ideas.

**Compliment family members** on their responsive interactions and the way they play with their child. Emphasize how important these interactions are for children's development. Encourage them to sing, cuddle, and engage with their infants during ongoing care routines and in play—every interaction is an opportunity for learning.

**Avoid making judgments** when you listen to families describe their caregiving practices, even if your approach is different. If you have a suggestion, share it as "Something that works here for us is . . ." rather than "This is the right way to do it." They are the most important people in their children's lives. Help them see that you honor and value that.

**Document children's experiences** and share with families the ways their children are growing and learning. Ask what wonderful things they see their children doing at home.

**Offer reassurance.** Many families are concerned about their children's development and their own competence at parenting. Reassure them and encourage them to just *be* with their child—to enjoy whatever it is that fascinates their little one right now and embrace those wonders together.

## Resources for Families

Various organizations provide information on child development that families may find helpful. Many list things families can do with a child at home, such as play peekaboo, offer a range of toys in a muffin tin, or create shakers out of discarded water bottles. Try to provide a variety of resources so that families can find the right ones for themselves. To start, see "Where to Find More" at the end of this chapter, which lists several resources and organizations.

# Document Children's Play and Learning

Document what children are learning as they play to highlight how important their play is. When you gather data on what children are doing and saying, you zero in on the key concepts and skills they're learning, and with this data you can focus on materials to present next. When you pair this with a tool such as the Desired Results Developmental Profile (California Department of Education 2015), which outlines key milestones over time, you can guide each child, building on his interest areas and strengthening skills that are less developed. The process of documentation is also extremely useful for your own and other staff members' professional development (Luckenbill 2012).

Here are some of the whats, hows, and whys of documentation.

### What and how to document

> Record anecdotes and take photographs that illustrate children's words, actions, and interests and show how they're expanding their skills as they play.

> Collect and display children's artwork. Toddler artwork may consist of blobs of dried playdough with craft sticks sticking out at various angles or scribbles of circles, dots, and lines. Infant artwork may be the mural paper used for group events like body painting and the photographs you take of these activities.

> Have your colleagues take photos or videos of your interactions with children.

### Why document

> Shows families how their child is developing and learning
> Gives families a window into the classroom community
> Provides ideas for similar play activities they can do at home
> Strengthens the home–school relationship
> Improves your own practice: looking at photos and videos of yourself interacting with children shows how you use your own face and body to engage them and suggests changes that could make your interactions more successful (like animating your face more when cheering a child's success or giving an infant a bit more time to take a turn when you're "talking" back and forth)

### How to share what you document

> Highlight the day's events with families at pickup time.
> Text or email anecdotes or photos to families during the day.
> Post children's art and photos of classroom experiences around the room and building.
> Provide print or digital newsletters that talk about what the children are doing, how they use the space, and why you provide certain materials and activities.
> Share the anecdotes, photos, and sample artwork you collect with families at conferences.

Your close, respectful relationships with young children and their families are the basis for playful interactions that support healthy growth and learning. As you observe children, plan experiences that enhance their individual development, narrate their actions and your own, and join in their play as a responsive partner, you encourage them to continue exploring and building their understanding of the world. As their competence and confidence grow, so do yours.

# Where to Find More:
## Resources for Teachers and Families

Child Care Aware of America: www.childcareaware.org

"Child Development": www.cdc.gov/ncbddd/childdevelopment/index.html

"Everyday Ways to Support Your Baby's and Toddler's Early Learning" (in English and Spanish): www.zerotothree.org/resources/265-everyday-ways-to-support-your-baby-s-and-toddler-s-early-learning

"Good Toys for Young Children by Age and Stage": NAEYC.org/resources/topics/play/toys

"How to Care for Infants and Toddlers in Groups": www.zerotothree.org/early-care-education/child-care/caring-for-infants-and-toddlers-in-groups.html

"Landscape for Learning: The Impact of Classroom Design on Infants and Toddlers," by L. Torelli and C. Durrett: www.earlychildhoodnews.com/earlychildhood/article_view.aspx?ArticleID=238

"Make the Most of Playtime": http://csefel.vanderbilt.edu/documents/make_the_most_of_playtime2.pdf

"Milestone Moments: Learn the Signs. Act Early.": www.cdc.gov/ncbddd/actearly/pdf/parents_pdfs/milestonemomentseng508.pdf

National Association for the Education of Young Children (NAEYC): NAEYC.org

"Play": www.zerotothree.org/early-learning/play

"Play Developmental Milestones": www.luriechildrens.org/en/specialties-conditions/pediatric-occupational-therapy/developmental-milestones/play-developmental-milestones

"Rocking and Rolling: Empowering Infants' and Toddlers' Learning Through Scaffolding," by L.G. Gillespie and J.D. Greenberg (*Young Children,* Vol. 72, No. 2, pp. 90–92, May 2017): NAEYC.org/resources/pubs/yc/may2017/rocking-and-rolling-empowering-infants-and-toddlers

"Why This Toy?," by S. Auerbach: NAEYC.org/our-work/families/why-this-toy

"Your Child's Development: Age-Based Tips From Birth to 36 Months": www.zerotothree.org/resources/series/your-child-s-development-age-based-tips-from-birth-to-36-months

ZERO TO THREE: www.zerotothree.org

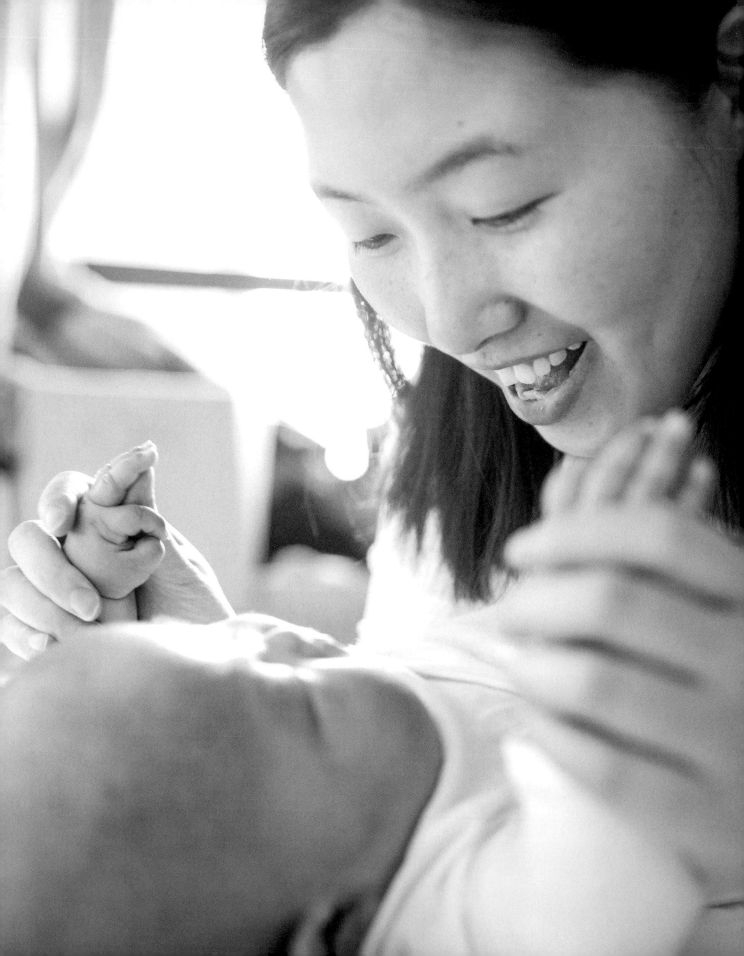

# 2

# The Young Infant:
## Birth to 9 Months

Young infants are at first mostly interested in you—your face, your expressions, your tone of voice. They gradually discover objects and other people around them.

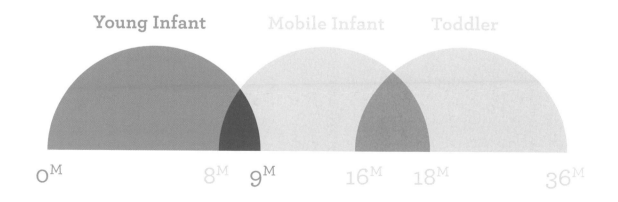

**Young Infant**   Mobile Infant   Toddler

0ᴹ   8ᴹ 9ᴹ   16ᴹ 18ᴹ   36ᴹ

# What's an Infant Like from Birth to 3 Months?

The very young infant is ready to meet the world and expects social interaction. A basic form of play in these early months is simply connecting and making eye contact with you. Moments when the two of you share attention are pleasurable for her. Soon, your smile or coo earns you a similar response from the infant, and you engage in back-and-forth circles of interaction together—a more complex form of play.

This infant explores the world using her senses and movement (Bornstein, Arterberry, & Lamb 2013). As she approaches 3 months of age, she loves mouthing items when she can get them to her mouth. She finds her hands to be quite entertaining! She focuses on objects that interest her, such as simple toys, for short periods of time. But she prefers you and other people to objects, gradually imitating your facial expressions and the sounds you make. She also enjoys following your movements.

She likes to be held so she can watch and imitate your facial expressions. At times, she gets overwhelmed by the attention and needs you to know when to look away and help her return to calm by rocking, singing, swaddling, and shushing (Karp 2015).

This Is Play

# What's an Infant Like at 3 to 6 Months?

As she becomes more alert and active, the young infant wants more interaction with the adults in her life. She deeply enjoys back-and-forth games with you and songs or chants with hand gestures. She uses her face and body to signal to you when she is ready for playful interactions, like touching your face and reaching toward your hair or glasses. She mirrors your expressions, uses more social smiles, and even laughs.

This infant can sit up for very brief times, with help, and is ready to explore the classroom in a different way than before. She may start rolling over from her back to her stomach, using this position to grasp toys that are nearby.

She's testing out how her body acts in relation to toys and people and how they respond. You'll see her mouthing, handling, banging, and shaking objects in an effort to understand what they are and what they do. She imitates the actions and sounds of others, which helps her learn new skills.

If you give her a toy like a set of fabric stacking rings with different colors, textures, and sounds, she may settle on a certain ring that makes a crunch sound and has small bumps—she's noticed these characteristics and selects this ring every time to mouth and handle. While you cannot know exactly what the infant is thinking, you can be sure that she is gathering information from each object she explores and each interaction she has.

# What's an Infant Like at 6 to 9 Months?

This infant is keenly interested in other people. She tries to engage her peers by reaching out to touch their hands and faces. Being more stable while sitting makes it easier for her to reach out, grasp, and handle toys. She might be working on learning to roll, scoot, or crawl to a location she likes.

She's figuring out where things are in space, grasping at hanging hair and ribbons, tracking items as they fall, and looking at things from various angles. She's noticing that actions cause things to happen. She focuses longer on a toy or activity that she enjoys, allowing her to learn more about the object or person that fascinates her—for example, you!

This Is Play

Young infants benefit from playful interactions and experiences that are tailored to their needs. As you get to know each infant, you'll discover who

> Likes listening to your voice or the voices of the other children
> Likes to look around at the objects in the room
> Wants to move, move, move!
> Enjoys lively social interactions
> Prefers low-key interactions

Carefully observing an infant's behavior will also give you a picture of his cognitive (thinking) skills, language, motor development, and social and emotional development. Then, putting together your understanding of where each infant is in his development with his unique personality and preferences, you can select toys and determine the kinds of interactions and play experiences that can best support and extend his development.

## What's a Teacher of Young Infants Like?

Working with young infants, you slow down and tune in. You watch for children's cues and ask yourself what they might need at that moment, then adapt, sometimes trying many things in the quest to understand. You are the calm in the storm, singing and rocking infants when they cannot soothe themselves. Then, as infants become ready to explore the playthings you offer, you shift to offering gentle play suggestions and become a coexplorer and facilitator of infants' discoveries during play!

## The Teacher's Role:
### Be Caring and Responsive

A young infant's work and play center around new people to engage with, new routines to learn, new spaces to see, new textures to feel, and new toys to explore. You'll strive to support him as he engages in these new experiences and learns to communicate. As you provide predictable routines and promote the young infant's feelings of warmth and security in the classroom, he will become more interested in playing with you.

# Getting to Know Each Other

Being a supportive play partner starts with observing and getting to know each infant and family.

**Learn each infant's cues.** Preferably this occurs gradually, with a visit to the family's home. If this is not possible, engage the family and the child together in the program before separation is necessary. That way you can see what routines are comfortable, what patterns of interaction are familiar, and what the infant likes and dislikes.

Pay attention to each child's cues so that you can follow, rather than lead, interactions. (See "Reading Young Infants' Cues to Plan Playful Interactions.") When you use your face, voice, or gestures, does the infant respond? If not, change your tone and expressions to make it more obvious that you are giving her cues to imitate you and join the interaction (Greenspan 1999).

**Gently engage.** Begin engaging the infant with quiet smiles, conversation, and if needed, playthings similar to the ones she prefers at home. Watch for her cues to know when she is ready to play and engage, such as making eye contact and cooing. Place yourself at the infant's level and engage her for brief periods of time with interactive play, like quiet songs and simple, soothing conversation. Continue as long as the infant is alert, engaged, and focused on your face.

**Give space for resting and refueling.** New experiences can be overwhelming, so if a baby seems overwhelmed by your face, voice, or gestures, tone down the interaction. Provide some recovery time when she needs a break: let her refuel by looking away, gazing at a wall, or sucking on her hands. Find a balance between being too intense or demanding, which can make her feel overwhelmed, and being too disengaged, which can make her feel lonely, sad, or afraid.

While some infants do tend to be fussier, their messages about their needs are valid. Respond in a way that will meet their needs at that moment. If an infant reengages after a while, continue to gently interact. If she continues to turns away, gazes at something else, yawns, flails, or arches her back, end the interaction. Over time, gradually extend your interactions with the infant.

As a young infant begins to move and explore more of the environment, you'll be a safe retreat for her—a place she can come back to when she needs comfort or recharging. Watch for these cues and respond warmly. Soon she'll be ready to explore again.

# Reading Young Infants' Cues to Plan Playful Interactions

It is important to understand each infant's cues in order to know when to play, when to stop and let him refuel, and when to focus on meeting the infant's other needs, such as hunger or discomfort. Invite families to share their infants' cues with you.

**Smiling.** Infants' first smiles generally appear between 6 and 8 weeks, usually in the context of physical comfort. Smiles tell you that the infant enjoys the play and social connection.

> *What to do:* Smile and comment: "You're smiling! You look so happy!"

**Imitating.** Between 3 and 6 months, most infants imitate facial expressions, not only smiles but also expressions of fear, surprise, and sadness. Remember that infants are reading *your* cues too. If you feel stressed, the infant will also (Waters, West, & Mendes 2014). Calm, playful interactions mean a great deal to infants.

> *What to do:* Imitate the noises, gestures, and expressions an infant makes. Try singing a song such as "Where Is Thumbkin?" and pause to see if the infant will coo or gesture a bit in response.

**Averting gaze.** From about 2 months onward, infants disconnect from interaction when they are overwhelmed or overstimulated (Stifter & Moyer 1991). You might see an infant turn away, play with his fingers or toes, or start crying to break the contact with an adult.

> *What to do:* Although it is tempting to get into the infant's line of sight, tickle, or jostle him back to attention, resist that temptation. Respect his need for downtime and wait quietly until he turns back and reengages in play.

**Rubbing his eyes or ears.** Infants will use their hands to rub their eyes and pull on their ears when tired. They may also rub their faces against something if they are tired or itchy.

> *What to do:* Stop the play and start the child's naptime routine.

**Startle reflex.** Loud noises, bright lights, or an unexpected jiggle of the infant's head can trigger the startle reflex—babies jerk, spread out their arms and legs, then quickly pull them back in and cry. The startle reflex is present at birth but fades between 3 and 6 months.

> *What to do:* Startling can happen when play is too abrupt. Calm the baby by rocking and speaking soothingly, and adapt your play to include more gradual movements.

(continued)

**Crying.** An infant cries when he has failed to communicate using subtler cues like turning away or arching his back. It is the quickest way for him to let you know that there is a problem. By 1 or 2 months of age, you may hear greater variation in an infant's cries, with even more variations over time. Some cries mean that infants have basic needs that are unmet, such as sleep, feeding, and pain.

*What to do:* Stop the play. The infant is overwhelmed or bored and may need a new activity, a break from play, or a physical need attended to. If you hear an **indecisive, bored, or overstimulated cry—**a staccato "ehh ehh ehh" cry—it will change to laughter if the infant is bored and you respond by interacting with him, or it might change to shrieks of anger if he feels overstimulated. Use other cues mentioned and the context of the situation to help you understand the message.

**Cooing, babbling, and laughing.** This "talk" begins around 2 or 3 months of age. You can hear infants copy your variations in pitch.

*What to do:* Be playful. Take turns as if you are talking with an adult (Bornstein, Arterberry, & Lamb 2013). Make the same noises back, then wait expectantly to see if the infant will take a turn.

When infants are content and attentive, they are ready to handle the stimulation that the world offers. Work with families to learn to recognize each infant's early stage cues— whining, pulling ears, rubbing eyes—that signal a need (sleep, food, diaper change, overstimulation) to which you should respond quickly and competently. This will help the baby relax enough to play and interact with you.

**Continue responsive interactions.** Young infants enjoy back-and-forth interactions with you. On occasion you can start these interactions, and at other times you can imitate the infant. This expands his "circles of communication" (Greenspan 1999)—a term for the practice of responsive interactions in which each player takes a turn and then waits for the other to take a turn, completing that "circle."

When you try to engage an infant, notice whether she responds with her own gestures or words to communicate back. If she does not, offer an activity you know she likes, such as peekaboo, or a few toys for her to choose from (Greenspan 1999). Give her feedback using your face, gestures, and voice. Comment enthusiastically on her attempts to communicate and on what she is doing.

## Communication circles with a 7-month-old

"Peekaboo!" grins teacher Trudi from behind a shelf. A huge, toothless smile spreads across 7-month-old Jack's face as he makes eye contact. Trudi ducks back, and Jack's face becomes serious. He stares at the shelf. "Peekaboo!" Trudi says again, and Jack responds with a grin and a gurgle.

Trudi knows that these circles of communication are important to Jack. It's not just play; it teaches him the turn-taking engagement pattern of adult conversation. When Jack's attention shifts to the contents of the shelf and he selects a small musical shaker to put in his mouth, Trudi shifts too, commenting, "That looks bumpy. You put it in your mouth!" Jack looks up and smiles again, and the circles continue.

As an infant becomes a little older, continue to respond quickly to her cues and communication attempts. If she is making sounds, look excited and wait for your turn to make sounds back to her. When you respond to an infant's message, you are saying to the infant that she is a competent communicator who deserves a response.

Use self-talk to let an infant know that you respect him as a person: "Jian, I'm going to pick you up now and take you to the changing table to change your diaper. Then you can play with the ball again." Self-talk also shows him how language is used to communicate and helps him understand what will happen next, so his language development and cognition get a boost from you when you use this technique.

It's not always easy to find time for these interactions in a busy infant room. Slip them in wherever you can, as Rita does:

## Making time to connect with each infant

Rita spends a lot of time talking to the four young infants in her care as she changes their diapers, feeds them, and puts them down for naps. She imitates their coos and gurgles, talks about what she is doing, and narrates what she sees them doing as they play. She offers them each several choices of objects to explore while she attends to one infant's physical care, being careful to prevent them from mouthing each other's toys.

## Supporting More Exploration

As an infant shifts from play that mainly involves you to exploring objects by mouthing, handling, shaking, and banging them, adapt your play techniques. Offer safe, appropriate toys and imitate the child's actions, such as shaking an object, to join him as he explores. For example, invite him to roll the fire truck back and forth. This expands his play skills and shows him how interactive play works.

Promote an infant's language development by commenting on the things he is doing: "I see you crawling to the basket. You're pulling the basket over!" Narrating stories and reading are also valuable, playful experiences. These activities introduce "rare" words—words that are a bit more complex or less commonly used in everyday speech—and build on the concepts that language is enjoyable and that print has meaning. For example, teacher Abigail comments to Griffin, "You're looking at the book *Slippery Fish in Hawaii!* That's a tuna fish you are looking at, and it's eating the octopus!"

**Infant "research": balancing challenges with safety.** Infants love discovering ways to make a big effect on their environment. They throw spoons off high chairs, bang on toy pianos, roll items around the room, and pull hair. They experiment with how things fit in different spaces by dumping out water from a container or taking everything out of the ball basket and then climbing in.

As infants build their understanding of cause and effect through experiences like these, they are better able to predict how the people and objects in their lives will respond to actions and interactions. So, set them up with opportunities where they can experiment with making things happen—in ways that work for you and keep everyone safe. Here are some ways you might redirect an infant's cause-and-effect research efforts:

> If an infant's drop-the-spoon game isn't right for the space, provide a ball drop where she can track balls as they fall down a tube.

> Redirect an infant who is pulling on your hair to dangling thick plastic loops of chain securely affixed to a bell on the ceiling—this lets the infant test cause and effect around pulling on things.

> For infants who want to play peekaboo when you need your hands free, offer things like securely attached curtains that are fun to crawl to and then peek from behind.

Be sure to acknowledge these experiments with positive words and a wide smile to show that you value children's learning and that it's safe to explore. When you create a safe environment for learning, you encourage play and exploration because you rarely need to say no or intervene to remove children from unsafe situations. This frees you to join their play in a relaxed and playful manner.

**Doing it my way: making choices.** Many young infants have preferences for what they want to play with and where. Infants who are beginning to move can go to the play location they prefer and select toys from shelves at their level. Keep toys in predictable areas of the room so these infants can find the items they like.

Infants who are not yet moving around on their own will likely need you to read their cues about what they want. Help the infant fulfill his intentions by figuring out where he is looking or what he is pointing to, then bringing him the item he seems interested in. Notice how Francis's teacher does this:

### A 7-month-old gets his book—with a little help

Francis (7 months) is seated below a shelf containing stacking cups. His gaze seems to be on the cups. His teacher, following the cue, reaches out and taps one. "It looks like you want this cup," she comments. He continues to stare. She looks again. Perhaps he's looking at the picture of a dog on a book above the cups. "Or this book?" she asks. Francis smiles as she takes the book down and hands it to him. He reaches out and grasps the book, staring more closely at the dog.

Be flexible if the infant uses an item in ways other than you expect. For example, if an infant gestures toward the whisk on the shelf and you take it down and hand it to him, you might model a whisking motion and offer a bowl for him to try doing it. But if he decides that what he really wants to do with the whisk is mouth it, adapt your response. Perhaps you comment on how the whisk feels. It's okay for infants to focus on objects of interest in the ways they research best.

Give the infant time and space to explore the item on his own. While he does so, you might take a moment to check on the other infants. The same infant who was intent on exploring the whisk on his own might later offer it to you, indicating he may want to rejoin social play. You might hand the whisk back and forth or grab and shake a second whisk with him to investigate how it moves in space.

As you see young infants learning and accomplishing more and more, introduce more complex experiences into the classroom. Add some scarves and tissue boxes or containers with items to mouth and dump. The infant's play may still seem very basic and repetitive (shaking, mouthing, handling, and banging), but now he is able to make choices about his explorations and will learn a great deal about the characteristics of the things he selects.

**Discovering peers.** As infants begin to move around and explore, an exciting development is their growing interest in each other. They grasp and poke things, including eyes and tufts of hair. Peers make such interesting noises when grasped! You can coach and guide these explorations by

> Naming an infant's action or situation
> Setting positive limits and redirecting children when needed

Notice how Carolina, a teacher, does this for Wing and Leah:

### Gentle touching with an 8- and 9-month-old

Leah (8 months) has been attending an infant program for two months. She smiles as her teacher, Carolina, greets her, and Leah reaches out her arms to be held. When placed on the floor next to Wing (9 months), Leah makes eye contact and smiles. Carolina smiles too and comments, "You are sitting with your friend, Leah!" Wing reaches over and strokes Leah's arm. "That was a gentle touch, Wing," comments Carolina as she gestures "gentle" by stroking her own arm. Wing reaches out her palm and gently strokes Carolina's arm too. "Very gentle," comments Carolina, smiling.

Be sure to comment when you see an infant acting gently with another child so she receives attention from her positive actions. Avoid stepping in only when the action gets upsetting. If an interaction is not positive, redirect a child to other activities or guide her to touch you (gently!) instead. In the scene above, Carolina encouraged further social interaction by commenting on the positive interaction rather than preventing Wing from touching Leah (Halle et al. 2011). Her sensitive response, which included both words and gestures, also added to the children's developing language skills.

## Understanding Infants' Uniqueness

As you spend time with each infant, you'll discover her unique personal style. Observe carefully to see how each child explores, what she prefers, how she interacts with others, and how she responds to the environment (Wanerman 2015). These preferences influence a child's behavior and interactions in play.

Knowing this, you can support even very young infants at play and create an environment and caregiving and teaching style that are a good fit for each child—meeting her particular needs and preferences. If you understand the impulse behind an infant's behavior, you can adapt your strategies to better fit the child and the situation. This helps you coach sensitively until the infant is successful at a task or interacting with others—without labeling her as "bad," "the aggressive one," or "the shy one."

**Infants who go with the flow.** Some infants adapt quickly to new settings and may show only mild reactions when their needs are unmet for a time. It can be easy to leave these infants in one location for too long or miss their more subtle cues while you are tending to infants who seem to need more of your attention. But like all infants, they need opportunities to engage in back-and-forth interactions with you in play.

**Infants who need some time to get used to new experiences.** You'll notice that some infants take a while before they are comfortable exploring. They may be hesitant to engage in new experiences and prefer to watch before play or meeting new people. Once comfortable, however, these children often willingly play and engage. Plan a gradual entry to play and interaction with other staff for them. Use pictures or words to explain what will happen next. For example, you might say, "Hi, Zaine! Today we have something new that I think you'll like to try—warm, soapy water! I'll take you over and we can look at it together." Give him plenty of time, if he needs it, to check it out visually, and gradually encourage him to touch it.

**Infants who react more strongly.** Some infants may show more intense emotional reactions and have difficulty with transitions, new situations, or unfamiliar people. Noise or other forms of sensory stimulation may easily upset them. Because of this, they may be less skilled in play interactions and need you to be a careful cue reader and sensitive supporter during interactions. Narrate what is happening as you care for these infants, and talk about play opportunities you are going to present before you present them. For example, you might say to Karoo (6 months), who is in your lap, "Karoo, I'm going to stand up!" Pause, then stand with him in your arms. "Now let's go over to the fish tank!" This area is calming to Karoo, and with only one other infant in that area quietly mouthing a plastic fish, you know that the noise level will not overwhelm Karoo.

**Be aware of your own reactions to each infant's style.** While you may have different approaches to situations and people than a particular child does, you can adapt your behavior to fit his preferences. This is important for supporting the infant's well-being and learning.

For example, you may have two infants the same age who join your group at the same time. One infant, Annette, cries when she is wrapped too tightly, hears loud sounds such as the vacuum cleaner, is in a brightly lit room, or is wiped during diapering. She does not like to be placed on the floor, and the slightest noise wakes her from sleep. In short, she is sensitive to many everyday stimuli in the classroom.

Sufen, however, almost never cries. She sleeps well, enjoys exploring objects while on her tummy, and smiles through diapering. You may find yourself preferring Sufen and seeking her out for interaction. And without realizing it, you may frown and tense when you go to place Annette on the floor to play because you know that she usually doesn't respond well when placed on the floor. If you pay close attention, you may find that you rarely engage in interpersonal play with Annette because much of your time together is spent attempting to calm her before and after care routines.

It would be tempting for you to privately feel that Annette is spoiled or difficult and that Sufen's family has made "better" choices about their caregiving and interacting than Annette's. But each family has adapted their routines and care to their child's unique makeup and responses.

Consider how you can do the same by adapting two things: the classroom (maybe fewer triggers for an infant who's sensitive) and your attitude. Deliberately focus on connecting with an infant. This requires mindfulness in caregiving routines and play interactions. Rather than view a child as being hard to work with, simply acknowledge that your personality and preferences are different from hers and look for ways to be more responsive to her needs. And celebrate successes!

**Infants with delays or disabilities.** When you work with children who have developmental delays or disabilities, look for their strengths and build on those rather than focus on what they can't yet do. It can be easy to get frustrated when a child seems to be making little progress, but that frustration on your face and in your voice can produce anxiety in the infant, leading to a negative interaction between the two of you.

Instead, look for activities that bring him pleasure and provide success, even though the success may be small or basic. Once the infant is more relaxed, address his developmental needs through targeted play interactions. For example, if you have an infant who is struggling to develop the muscles to stay in a seated position, providing a lap or pillow opposite a new toy or a mirror invites practicing the skill of sitting, even for just a few moments, while also cushioning his eventual fall from this position. Also, seek information from any early intervention professionals working with the child.

# An Engaging Environment for Young Infants: Simple and Soothing

Setting up the environment to support infants' growing exploration and learning takes some careful thought. You must balance safety with challenge, children's interests, and your available space and materials.

## What Do Play Areas Look Like?

**Inviting and restful.** The infant classroom should be homelike. When considering toys, materials, equipment, wall colors, or decoration, ask yourself, "Is this necessary and productive stimulation? Do the sights, sounds, and textures advance the children's learning? Do toys, photos, books, and other materials reflect the cultures of the children and families here? How can we simplify the environment?"

Very young infants are likely to be easily overwhelmed by what's around them, so limit background music, busy patterns and other visual distractions, electronic toys, and similar stimulation. Although it may seem less friendly, walls with few images or mobiles are more restful for young infants' eyes than walls that have many images and bright colors. Infants need rest to refuel and return to play interactions.

**Clutter-free spaces for exploring.** Arrange the room so infants can focus on their preferred play choices. A young infant's head and limbs are often in motion, so give him space to move. When you place him in play spaces, keep in mind that from one day to the next, he may be more able to flip, roll, and grasp things. Watch for unsafe objects and locations he might encounter. Outdoors, young infants benefit from lying on a blanket or being held by a teacher, enjoying the trees moving above them and other sights, sounds, and smells.

Support infants' emerging abilities to explore the items in the classroom. For example, at 4 months when most infants have enough head and upper body control, being placed seated in a wading pool lined with a quilt beside a basket with a few types of rattles and balls might be perfect. But a few months later, the same infant may want to be placed near the climber, with an inclined ramp leading up to a basket of balls, and invited to crawl to the top. Keep in mind that the things that are exciting one week may be old news by the next week—or not! Some groups of infants "ask" to keep a specific toy, such as a ball pit, for many months by showing continued interest in the materials and gravitating toward that area.

**A selection of toys where infants can reach them.** Infants who are reaching and grasping and selecting toys will enjoy treasure baskets. Gather a few items from various areas of the room that you know a particular child might be interested in, like measuring spoons (interesting to handle and mouth), a wooden rattle, several blocks with transparent centers inviting peekaboo, a cloth book, and a bumpy plastic ball. Place the items in a basket and put the basket where the infant will discover it—perhaps on a safe space on a mat near the child.

Treasure baskets give the infant choices in his play and give him a chance to learn about a variety of materials, even if he is not yet moving around on his own. Change the basket contents based on the infant's preferences.

**Items on reachable shelves.** Young infants also enjoy being placed in areas of the classroom near low shelves with clear choices displayed on them. Again, periodically rotate the items in them to invite new explorations.

Of course, play with young infants takes place everywhere in the room and during caregiving routines. Take advantage of play and learning opportunities with your captive audience during diapering, feeding, and other routines, like exploring food textures at mealtime.

## Ideas for Play at Home

Young infants are entertaining to play with in the home setting. You can share lists of simple activities that family members can do with their infants, such as creating homemade rattles, sorting toys in muffin tins, rolling a ball, splashing in a tub of water, and banging on a drum. Ask families what games they enjoy playing with their infants at home, and use these as a way to bring children's home cultures into the classroom.

**Items grouped together.** When designing the classroom for infants who are beginning to explore more, try grouping together materials that encourage particular types of play and learning. For example, depending on available space and the infants' interests and skills, you might have a quiet area, a more active area, a place for exploring sensory materials, and a music area. See "Spaces and Play Materials for Infants Striking Out on Their Own" on pages 42–47 for more suggestions on arranging spaces and choosing items for each area.

# What Do Young Infants Play With?

**Items for early exploration.** A very young infant's first play materials are simple: her own body and yours. She explores with cries, coos, and the aimless wandering of arms and legs in the air, followed by gazing, batting, and grasping.

It is more important for you to hold, sing to, and talk to newborns than to hand them a toy. In fact, "infants need touch and physical contact with teachers in order to grow and thrive" (Gross 2008, 192). When you are not holding an infant, make sure that she is in a place where she can still feel a part of the group but where more active infants will not run her over.

As a teacher of young infants, *you* are their favorite plaything! As infants become comfortable in the classroom and more connected to you, expect to see playful interactions. These interactions will vary widely with developmental progress and personality, even within a group of similarly aged children. Watch carefully for an infant's invitation to play—it may be very subtle, like shaking his hand in the air or grasping a strand of your hair. Or it could be more obvious, like hiding his face to "ask" for a round of peekaboo.

**Things to bat and grasp.** For infants who cannot yet release their grasp on toys when the toys are placed in their hands, batting at hanging items may be more satisfying than handheld toys. When the infant is on her back, hang toys above her mat or from the ceiling that she can kick with her feet, bat at, and later grasp and pull. (Teachers must closely supervise an infant playing with toys with cords once the infant gains skill at pulling!) These toys often make noise, have an interesting texture, or include a simple, bold pattern, helping the infant learn about the sights and sounds of things around her.

Once an infant gains control of her hands, offer small lightweight, slender rattles or textured or crinkly toys and books. These are better choices than large, heavy, or complex toys.

**Things to look at.** Choose books and pictures with images infants find intriguing. Some very young infants prefer to look at black-and-white bold images that look like faces over other kinds of images. You can print, draw, or purchase these kinds of images. Other ideas to consider include famous artworks on the walls, mobiles that move in the breeze, fish in a fish tank, and a plant or bouquet of flowers on the counter.

**Things to manipulate and combine.** Offer toys to further infants' investigations of how things work, like fabric animals, rings, blocks, and rattles of many shapes, textures, and sizes. Infants also enjoy handling dolls and props for the dolls, like hats, cups, and spoons.

As infants gain skill and attention, they shift from simply examining the characteristics of an object with their senses to using two objects together (Gerber, Wilks, & Erdie-Lalena 2010). Provide objects for infants to bang together, manipulate, and dump, such as sorting boxes containing just a few shapes, tissue boxes filled with scarves to pull out, and blocks of various shapes and sizes. Stay nearby and comment on their play activities—you'll help them feel safe to take these small risks and learn about sounds, textures, and what they can do with more complex items.

**Finding play items.** You can scavenge wonderful playthings for infants at secondhand stores (be sure to inspect them for sharp or broken edges). Cooking spoons, spatulas, bowls, and muffin tins are interesting to handle. Discarded cloth bags and clothing can be washed, cut up, and then sewn together to make fabric texture books. Baskets, boxes, and bins can be used for filling and dumping. Things you may want to purchase new include diverse baby dolls and books showing a diversity of people. Used versions of these are sometimes harder to find.

## Safety Note

All mouthed toys must be sanitized between uses by different infants, so choose toys that can stand up to frequent cleanings (see "Where to Find More" at the end of this chapter for an NAEYC resource on cleaning and sanitizing). As with all household or everyday items you offer children (like metal whisks), examine them first to be sure they have no sharp parts. Use a choke tube to determine whether small toys are safe for the infant to play with.

## Spaces and Play Materials for Infants Striking Out on Their Own

For infants who are starting to explore on their own more, and particularly if infants stay in your room once they are mobile, you might group similar play items like blocks or musical items together in the room. Think about what the infants in your group like to do and what materials and experiences will enhance their cognitive, movement, and language skills. Keep the areas few and simple based on the space you have. If space is limited, items can simply be arranged on low shelves or in treasure baskets. Expect that infants will explore the items in different ways than older infants and toddlers will.

Change the contents of the spaces gradually and in ways that support the infants' interests. Unlike active toddlers, who may quickly tire of the same materials, young infants can enjoy the same activity or concept for a long period of time if you make just small changes.

For example, change the types of plastic produce or the size of bowls. Add some shakers that are heavier, smaller, or louder rather than replace all the instruments with different ones. Or change maracas to shakers made from water bottles. Bring in a higher ramp or add a new tunnel.

Every once in a while you can make a larger change. But when you do this, keep the other areas the same for the time being. This keeps the room feeling predictable and familiar as infants gradually expand their ability to remember people and information and for those who feel more comfortable when their surroundings are familiar.

**Active area.** Young infants stretch their arm muscles and torso a lot, so the ground in this area should be firm, allowing traction so infants can move themselves along without slipping.

> Use mats and locate active areas away from other equipment if there is a chance that infants could fall.
> Place low ramps for infants to crawl up and down and a central tunnel to crawl through.

## Safety Note

Be sure to secure all furniture so there is no danger of a bookcase or other item falling onto infants as they climb and explore.

**Quiet space.** Create a soft place with a few stuffed animals, pillows, and books, located away from more active spaces.

> Provide stuffed animals and other items that reflect the infants' homes and lives—for example, pets such as cats, dogs, or fish.
> Offer lots of books for infants to expand language and communicate interest in the names of things. You don't need to read entire books. Instead, respond to a child's cues: Is he looking at an image? Label it for him. It's okay for infants to handle, mouth, and bang books as they would any other toy. Redirect the infant to a teether if he is damaging the book.
> Be sure to wash linens regularly and any mouthed items before the next infant uses them.

**Block play.** Keep just a few items on a low shelf for infants who are exploring more. They are not yet stacking blocks and find clutter to be overwhelming.

> Place a few blocks for banging.
> Include a few accessories such as vehicles, toy trees, or plastic people large enough for safe mouthing and handling.
> Keep replacement items nearby so that when you remove mouthed items for washing, you can stock the shelves with more clean items. One infant can quickly deplete the entire selection of materials in an area! This balance between providing enough materials to explore and keeping the space uncluttered is important.

**Sensory play.** Since infants learn through all their senses, sensory play happens all day long in the infant program. You might also have an area where they can explore more unusual sensory materials; see examples below. Young infants will mouth, eat, or drink any sensory materials, so you must supervise them closely when they're exploring. Place a mat under the space to make cleanup easier and to absorb splashes.

> For infants 6 months and older, provide nontoxic, open-ended materials to explore, such as a small bin of water with cups or a bin with crumpled newspaper. Offer a bin of finger paint (made with cornstarch and water, cooked a bit, with food coloring added).
> Use low containers such as those pictured to provide access to everyone, keep the materials safe and confined, and decrease mess.
> Have tools on hand—a trash can, broom and dustpan, wet wipes, towels, and teethers—so you can quietly redirect infants when needed and allow them to explore as much as possible with little negativity from adults.

This Is Play

## Sensory Play for Young Infants

Why invite such young infants to explore sensory materials? It helps them adapt to their environment, cope with different sensations on their hands and body, and learn motor and balance skills like how hard to lean in or bang on something to get results. As infants explore the feel of things on their hands, experience how water changes when moved gently or vigorously, and discover things that feel sticky or wet, they're also learning the foundations of math and science. They also gain language as you talk about the textures and other properties they're experiencing. At mealtime, for example, attach some words to the way an avocado might feel to an infant who is squeezing it between her fingers (squishy, slimy, warm). Infants' sensory play is the beginning of an exciting lifelong journey of discovering how materials work and how they can be combined.

**Cognitive play.** While infants learn from all types of materials, include items that support their thinking skills—like cause and effect, classifying, and solving problems.

> Provide shakers with unique sounds, weights, textures, and shapes. Offer happy little surprises in this area by changing the shakers every now and then. Infants will be intrigued—what will the new shakers do?

> Offer objects like stacking rings and stacking turtle-shaped toys that invite infants to consider size and shape, how objects are the same and how they are different, and how objects relate to each other (on top of, off, etc.) (Erikson Institute Early Math Collaborative, n.d.).

> Include baskets of several items that infants can dump. This activity may seem basic, but it invites infants to consider volume, delight in cause-and-effect play, and examine the concept of change—the basket was full, but now it is empty!

**Nature and science exploration.** Items from nature offer interesting opportunities for exploring, comparing, and learning about categories.

> Select natural items that have different textures (e.g., clean wool or scented bumpy items such as dried citrus fruits), hard items like large seashells and clean stones that are too heavy to throw, and rough items like closed pine cones.

> Draw infants' attention to the objects' characteristics and use words to describe what they're experiencing. As infants explore the textures, they begin to notice the similarities and differences and develop categories for the things around them, an important early mathematical skill.

> Include more unusual nontoxic materials, such as pumpkins and gourds, for infants to handle and mouth. Carefully watch infants who have teeth—they may try to take a bite out of one of these items.

Always consider safety when you set up spaces for young infants. Avoid items that can break apart into choking components, cut children with sharp edges, or harm them with splinters.

**Music space.** Include a range of musical items, inviting infants to make noise and express themselves.

> Small, lightweight musical instruments like shaker eggs are popular with very young infants because they are easy to grasp and handle. Try maracas, toy pianos, and drums.

> Provide books with musical themes, such as "Old MacDonald Had a Farm" or "Twinkle, Twinkle, Little Star" to help infants communicate their interest in songs as they hand you a book to sing along with.

**Family area.** Consider creating a familiar-feeling spot where infants can explore materials like those found in their homes. Knowing the families well will help you find appropriate items.

> Invite infants to explore real (but safe) tools such as whisks, pots, and measuring spoons, plastic food and flatware, and diverse dolls (see "Where to Find More").

> Post images of families of all types engaging in daily living tasks, including those of people doing non-gender-stereotyped activities, like men changing diapers. These invite infants to connect the play to real life, expanding their understanding of daily routines.

As you set up the room and plan for interactions with the infants, remember that infants rarely use the materials in the way you intended—and that's okay. Joining them by handling the same toys as you sit beside them and cooing or commenting may not seem like you are doing much playing, but it is a great gift. You are helping them form an understanding of the back-and-forth nature of conversation, showing them that their ideas have value, and inviting them to feel safe as they explore the world around them.

# Where to Find More:
## Resources for Teachers and Families

*California Infant/Toddler Learning & Development Foundations* (California Department of Education and WestEd, 2009): www.cde.ca.gov/sp/cd/re/documents/itfoundations2009.pdf

"Cleaning, Sanitizing, and Disinfection Frequency Table": NAEYC.org/sites/default/files /globally-shared/downloads/PDFs/accreditation/early-learning/clean_table.pdf

*A High-Quality Program for Your Infant* (NAEYC, 2017)

Lots to Love baby dolls (8–10 inches; diverse line of dolls that fit in toy wheelchairs, are small enough for infants to lift, and can stand up to mouthing): Available from manufacturer, JC Toys, and other online retailers

"Tips on Temperament": www.zerotothree.org/resources/243-tips-on-temperament

"Using Toys to Support Infant-Toddler Learning and Development," by G. Guyton: https://educate .bankstreet.edu/cgi/viewcontent.cgi?article=1006&context=faculty-staff

*The What, Why, and How of High-Quality Programs for Infants: The Guide for Families* (NAEYC, 2016)

# 3

# The Mobile Infant:
## 8 to 18 Months

The mobile infant, particularly as he gets further past his first birthday, is engaging in play that looks like play to most adults. He enthusiastically puts a toy person in a car or a spoon in a cup (relational play) and builds a tunnel for his car to go through (constructive play).

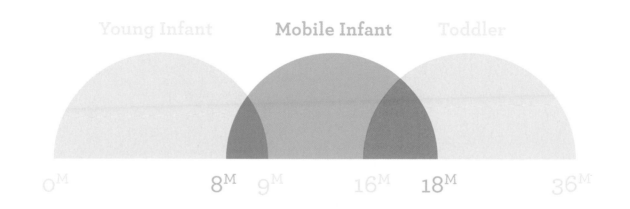

Young Infant     Mobile Infant     Toddler

0ᴹ     8ᴹ 9ᴹ     16ᴹ     18ᴹ     36ᴹ

# What's an Infant Like at 8 to 12 Months?

The 8- to 12-month-old infant is interested in everything. He's excited to understand the world and interact with others, although still anxious about strangers and novel situations. He reaches out to touch other infants. He loves to imitate your actions and sounds. He moves from joy at his newfound abilities to fear in novel situations and people to anger when he is prevented from trying new activities.

The young mobile infant can sit steadily, freeing his hands to focus on tasks like banging two objects together. His more accurate grasp allows him to successfully use toys to explore cause and effect—for example, by placing a ring on a stick, banging on drums, or smearing paint.

He may roll, crawl, scoot, pull up to stand, coast along shelving units or railings by walking in a sideways manner or gripping the rail, or take his first steps. This new mobility creates exciting opportunities for exploration and learning, as he can now move away from the treasure baskets or objects placed beside him and seek out interesting activity areas on his own. He may even reach materials on higher shelves. (Be sure the room is childproofed!)

Although he may prefer certain toys, this infant also is busy examining more intentionally how novel items work and what they do, like dumping and filling containers, pulling on strings, and pushing buttons. Repeating these actions over and over again deepens his understanding and gets him ready to learn more complex skills. You'll observe him solving problems by moving around obstacles in the classroom to reach a toy he wants or using tools like a shovel to fill a bucket.

He is learning to cope with delayed gratification—for example, having to wait to play until after his diaper is changed. He babbles with sounds in his home language that sound more and more like words, such as "Dada" or "Tatay" or "ba(ll)." He looks to you and the way you respond to him to learn that he is someone who can make change in his world (Mahler, Pine, & Bergman 1975) and to find validation of his emerging skills.

# What's an Infant Like at 12 to 18 Months?

As the mobile infant gains more skills, his play becomes more complex because he can grasp a crayon or a paintbrush to make marks and carry items over to fill a cart. He may sit on a scooter and move it backward or forward.

This child may enjoy simple puzzles, such as placing round bead-like puzzle pieces on rods and placing small boxes in large boxes. He likes to push buttons on pop-up toys to see what happens. While his play is basic—he tries things you know won't work, like trying to fit a big box into a small box—these problem-solving experiments are exciting because they are different and more complex than his earlier play in which he explored things mainly by banging, mouthing, and shaking them.

While this infant often plays with objects by himself, he also seeks out social games and interactions that involve repetition, such as peekaboo, so big, and where's the baby? He continues to be interested in children he's familiar with.

He communicates clearly, with gestures, facial expressions, and some first words in his home language (*ani/no, más/more, all done*). He enjoys back-and-forth communication with you and is likely to point out something to share it with you. For example, he might bring you a fish puppet, call it by name or use a gesture for "fish," and then hum the tune to the song "Octopus," by Charlotte Diamond, inviting a playful interaction.

This infant enjoys looking through books and may label the images he sees, though he may not want to sit through the entire book.

You will see an increase in both humorous interactions with grown-ups and peers (such as putting silly things on his head or climbing into tiny containers) and challenging behaviors when he is denied something or during transitions. This infant may take toys from other children, then show surprise when they protest!

You will see the older mobile infant using more overt problem solving in play—an exciting development. He is likely to see a puzzle or a bucket with a shovel as an invitation to action, and you will see him use these items in more expected ways.

He may also become frustrated when objects don't behave as he thinks they should, or when he does not have the motor skills to control the outcome. For example, he may be able to fit only the round puzzle piece in the hole and may bang on the triangular hole. He may not focus on one thing for long and is likely to leave you with a toy or activity, explore something else he likes, and then wander back to check in with you.

The mobile infant is an exciting mix of adventurer and seeker of close comfort. He wants to try out his new mobility and dexterity and seeks things out of sight. These same emerging abilities sometimes overwhelm him, as do changes in routines and new faces, and he may rapidly make a beeline back to you. The young mobile infant requires you to provide close supervision as he tries out his developing motor skills.

## What's a Teacher of Mobile Infants Like?

Working with mobile infants means you have empathy for babies in big-kid bodies. You are able to think and act quickly and to think ahead to prevent play mishaps. You can also slow down to notice small details with infants, such as ants on the sidewalk. You look at situations from many perspectives to help children navigate social challenges as they play.

You avoid being offended when the 1-year-old rebels against your authority, and you think of quick, playful options for redirection. You demonstrate patience—so much patience!—and allow lots of time for children to try new skills during play, such as putting on boots.

You're a good listener and keen observer of children's attempts to communicate using language and nonverbal cues. You're also a good communicator, giving clear directions and inventing songs, gestures, and finger plays that invite infants to be playful with language.

If your classroom includes children who are learning more than one language, you learn and use a few words or a simple song in their home languages that can be paired with play and routines. You show children that their home culture and languages are valued, as Mimi's teacher does below, which can help them feel secure so they can play and explore.

### Valuing a 13-month-old's home language

> Dual language learner Mimi (13 months) is standing at the sink, watching as her teacher guides another child's hands into the water and sings, "Washing, washing, washing Leo's hands . . ." When it is Mimi's turn, her teacher, knowing Spanish is her home language, guides her hands into the water and sings, "Lavamos, lavamos, lavamos las manos . . ." and then "Secamos, secamos, secamos las manos . . ." when she takes Mimi's hands out of the water. Later, as Mimi holds a block to her face, her teacher comments, "Te vco, I see you!"

You love to read books with children, yet you are willing to stop midway through a story to discuss the images on the page or to switch to a new play activity and leave the book for another time.

You capably navigate the sometimes chaotic room of tiny beings who do not yet have the benefit of much logic while staying calm and rational and playful. What a person!

When you do these things, what magic you can create in your classroom community. And how much power you have to help shape children's futures and the ways they interact, communicate, creatively solve problems, and cope with disappointments. It's a gift to be a teacher of children this age.

# The Teacher's Role:
## Provide a Safe Environment for Exploring

Infants' increasing abilities to move around on their own and communicate more will make this age both challenging and exciting for you. The infant's personality is emerging! You will need to adjust your own play techniques to accommodate his growing skills and scaffold his development to new levels.

## Easing Separation, Entering Play

Part of your role in the classroom is to continue as a secure base for mobile infants when their family members leave. Separation anxiety can be so intense that it's hard to ignore, and what you do to support a child—singing, reading, and so on—will help her feel comfortable enough to play as she adjusts to the classroom and the schedule.

Infants who experience anxiety when a beloved family member leaves need reassurance, predictability, and coping tools (Balaban 2011) before they can play and interact in the classroom:

### Using a ritual to help an 11-month-old settle in

Claude (11 months) smiles when he joins the children in the infant room but cries when his father leaves. His teacher doesn't take this personally. She rocks him and says soothingly, "Your papa will be back after circle time. He always comes back." She carries Claude to the fish tank because she knows he enjoys watching the fish. As she sings to him about the fish, Claude gradually relaxes in her arms, and soon his teacher puts him down to play with the other infants.

Try these strategies to help mobile infants ease into the routine of your classroom:

> Encourage family members to say goodbye to their infant rather than sneak out. This helps the infant feel she can trust her family and the classroom space.

> Help the infant feel that the space is safe for exploration by using a predictable routine or ritual, like visiting the fish tank or reading a book together, going to an area of the room that she enjoys playing in, or looking together out the window at the squirrels. The ritual or routine is usually unique to each child, and families can help decide which one works best for their child. Your calm, soothing tone along with the predictability of the routine helps infants feel safe.

> Invite the infant to engage in an activity you know she enjoys: "Let's play ball while we wait for Nana to come back. You loved playing with the ball yesterday."

> If the infant has a special comfort object, keep it somewhere handy but out of the reach of other children.

> Provide images of absent family members for the infant to look at to ease her distress.

As infants shift from easygoing explorers to strong opinion holders, you shift with them. Offer increasingly complex experiences that let them explore and solve problems, and provide social coaching as conflicts begin to occur over possessions. With more mobility, children are also expanding their gross motor (or rough-and-tumble) play, requiring you to be vigilant about their safety. Here are some suggestions for supporting the play of mobile infants.

## Tune In to Infants' Play and Emerging Skills

The 1-year-old wants you to tune in and play with him! When you pay attention and respond to his attempts at play, like picking up a spoon he dropped intentionally, you let him know that his ideas are worth exploring. He understands now that social interactions require back-and-forth engagement, and your patient willingness to repeat his play themes, such as peekaboo, allow him to practice turn taking.

### Responding to a 13-month-old's play bid

Carlos (13 months) ducks behind the table in the dramatic play area. His teacher, Brandon, reads his cues and ducks down too, with a huge grin. Then Brandon calls out to another infant who is nearby: "Kianna, where's Carlos?" Carlos pops up with a grin. "We see you! Peekaboo!" Brandon exclaims. Both infants duck down, and Brandon patiently repeats the game over and over.

## Talk About the Action and Show Excitement

Rather than coach a child to play with toys as an adult might play with them, simply explore the toys with the child and comment on what he is doing. If the child approaches a basket of puppets, get on his level. Be responsive and engaged—show on your face that you are interested and excited about his emerging skills as he examines each puppet.

Infants at this age take cues from their teachers to determine how they should feel about themselves. When you are engaged and excited about their interests and discoveries, you're showing them that their achievements are worthwhile. You're also supporting their feelings of self-worth.

**Keep using self-talk and parallel talk.** The techniques of self-talk and parallel talk that you used when the infant was younger are still important. Talking about what *you* are doing makes you seem predictable and safe when an experience might seem scary. Detailing what the *child* is doing expands his vocabulary and reassures him that you are giving him your attention. It may seem that you are talking to yourself, but infants are gathering and processing everything going on around them, and soon language will come pouring out!

**Let the child lead, and sometimes model to encourage new play.** It's important to focus primarily on observing the infant and what she appears to be interested in doing with a toy and to let her lead the way. However, you can model how you might use a toy that is similar to the one the infant is exploring. This may encourage her to imitate your actions and try something new.

Modeling is different from showing how to do something, so when modeling, don't insist that the infant watch and imitate. Merely use a toy similar to one she has and do something different with it. For example, if she's beating on a coffee can or oatmeal tub drum, grab another one and make a different rhythm, or beat it more softly or loudly. If the infant seems frustrated by a task, make it a little easier for her to accomplish—or coach her by offering tips about how to make a change that might help. For example, you can say, "It looks like you want to grab the ribbon for that bell pull, but it's swinging. I wonder what might happen if you wait until it stops and then grab it?" or "It looks like you rode your car into the wall. Maybe you can get off and turn it, and then get back on to make it move?"

You can model gestures and language, too. Use gestures along with words to give a child a way to express himself while his verbal language is still emerging. This can help decrease frustration he may feel and increase his sense of engaging in reciprocal communication with you (Kirk et al. 2012).

## Expand Children's Abilities to Follow Directions and Take Turns

Back-and-forth games strengthen children's cognitive skills as well as their language skills; taking turns is central to communication.

> Play a game like "I roll the ball to Micah; he rolls the ball to me."
> Sing and invite infants to gesture along with a song such as "Where, oh where, oh where is Asia? There she is!" Encourage infants to point to their friends as a way to create community through playful interaction. "Willoughby wallaby woo, an elephant sat on you. Willoughby wallaby womar, an elephant sat on Omar" is a puppet song that teaches names in a playful and musical manner.
> Tell simple stories with puppets who hide and need to be found: "Where is Mr. Meepers? Can you find him?"

## Provide a "Yes" Space and Offer Acceptable Choices

Mobile infants are curious, social, and capable, so they're exploring more—and often find themselves moving into territory that is off limits. To make their experiences more rewarding and keep your need to set limits to a minimum, provide a "yes" space, in which everything at the children's height is okay for them to explore (Lally, Stewart, & Greenwald 2009).

Similarly, when an infant displays challenging behavior, look for the need behind the behavior. The infant is telling you something. When you understand that need, you can redirect her to an acceptable choice. This generally works better than disciplining, especially if done through play.

For example, if an infant is throwing hard objects, hand her some soft ones and model throwing them at a large basket while saying firmly, "We throw soft things." This meets the infant's need to throw and keeps the other children safe. If an infant is pulling hair, take her over to a bell pull (cut so that it is just the length to grasp the ribbon or scarf but not long enough to wrap around anyone) and say, "This is something you can pull, but pulling hair hurts," and join her in ringing the bell. You're teaching her social skills while keeping in mind her need to explore and observe the effects of her own actions.

If you offer many opportunities for an infant to choose what she is interested in during interactions where there are many acceptable choices, there may be fewer power struggles when there is no choice—for example, when her diaper must be changed. With fewer power struggles, you both have more time and energy for play. Even when children do not have a choice of whether to do the activity, you can still make the experience playful, as Ozzie's teacher does:

### Playful routines for a 14-month-old

Ozzie (14 months) loves climbing, playing side by side with Zach (14 months), and engaging an adult by handing his teacher a plastic vehicle and then rolling the vehicles together along the edge of the loft in the classroom. When his teacher needs to change Ozzie's diaper, he resists, wanting to continue his play. His teacher is playful, flying him to the changing area like an airplane, and she sings about airplanes as she changes his diaper. Soon he is laughing along with her. Back on the floor, he eagerly resumes his play with Zach.

## Supporting Play with a Child Who Is Withdrawn

While you generally follow the lead of a child, accepting a play bid or modeling a play idea, there are instances when you might play *for* a child to invite her to feel safe enough to play along. Here's an example.

### Becca

Becca joined the center when she was 15 months old. Her mother suffers from severe depression and experienced domestic abuse. The staff works closely with Becca's mother, arranging support and helping find respite care. Becca's behavior in the classroom is changeable, reflecting how her mother is doing. When her mother is depressed, Becca looks sad and curls up on the floor in a fetal position, unresponsive to teachers. She often will not play.

Staff provide *time in* (see page 61) for Becca by reading books, cuddling, and singing with her. They offer props for Becca to act out the situations that are stressful to her and books that reflect her single-parent family structure. When Becca is withdrawn, they pick up Becca's preferred toys and pretend to play with them as a way to spark her interest. When Becca is more animated, they observe her closely to understand her passions and interests so they can help her find coping tools on days that are more difficult for her.

## Help Children Solve Problems with Materials

Mobile infants are great at observing and imitating, and they use these skills to help them learn how things work. As they grow and gain experience, they try several different strategies to get an object to do something. To build on and expand an infant's interest in problem solving, provide materials and experiences that are open ended. For example, join him in play in the music area with pianos, shakers, and drums. As you explore making music side by side, he can test out cause and effect, discover how to make different kinds of noises, and imitate your techniques, such as using rhythm to create a basic pattern.

In the art and sensory area, provide water and sand play tools as another way to invite this kind of play. Items in the cognitive area such as puzzles, lock boxes, nesting cups, and giant pop-beads are also great for problem solving. Avoid the temptation to correct something the child is doing, like trying to fit a larger cup into a smaller one. Let him try his own strategies, and if he begins to let you know that he is frustrated, then offer suggestions to help with the challenge.

### Helping a 15-month-old find a solution to the ball drop

Milo (15 months) picks up a rubber ball and tries to press it on the top of the ball drop box. The ball does not quite fit in. Milo's teacher, Daniel, comments, "You are pressing that big ball against the small hole . . . doesn't look like it's going in. I wonder why?" When Milo furrows his forehead and turns to Daniel, Daniel suggests, "Would you like to try my ball? It's smaller." He holds out a ball that will fit. By drawing Milo's attention to size differences and suggesting rather than insisting that he try a different way to solve the problem, Daniel has given Milo a way to succeed and to think about how to accomplish his goal the next time.

## Facilitate Social Interactions

**Understand why infants act as they do.** If you work with the same infants over time, you may see once mild-mannered infants begin to take toys from others, hit, and refuse to share materials and even space. This is not unusual as they start to have a plan in mind for their play. When a child needs certain materials to complete his play idea, he has more reason to declare a space his, seek to maintain control of props, and take what he feels he needs. Engaging in physical or impulsive behavior should not be taken to mean that children are bullies.

Infants may hand toys to other children, but they are not actually sharing. They may take the toys back at any time, and sometimes they just want to show someone an item. They are not ready to play with both the item and another infant at the same time, and they are not regressing when they suddenly decide to hoard all the items in the room as a play activity. View an infant's need for possession as a new stage rather than a regression. This helps you support the child in beginning to take turns, wait, and find other activities rather than be frustrated with the child for not using social skills that he is still working to develop.

**Use steps to help resolve social conflicts.** You can guide infants to make positive social choices and have smoother interactions. When a child is upset because another child needs the same toy, move close to the children involved, hold the disputed object with the children, identify the problem and the emotions it seems to be raising, and offer a solution, following through if necessary (Evans 2016). Notice how JiYoung uses this process with Elmo and Sandy:

### Resolving a conflict with a 12- and 15-month-old

> Elmo (12 months) is seated on the carpet in the cognitive area, handling a stacking cup. Sandy (15 months) walks up to him and grasps the cup. Elmo cries out. Sandy's teacher, JiYoung, has been observing the interaction. She comes over and holds the cup too, commenting, "The cup is in Elmo's hands, Sandy. He is using it. When you pull it, he looks sad." The teacher gestures "sad" by drawing a tear on her own cheek with her index finger.

> Sandy gestures "more," tapping her fingertips together. "Yes, that's a good idea," JiYoung comments brightly. "We can find more cups and let Elmo use this one! Let's go find more." She gestures "more" as she says the word. Sandy and JiYoung release the cup to Elmo, who relaxes. Sandy and JiYoung walk to the shelf and locate more cups. "Now you both have cups. We solved the problem," explains JiYoung.

Generally, appropriate solutions at this age include waiting and finding more toys. Taking turns involves more skill than is typically available at this age. Sharing—using the same toy together at the same time with a common goal—is possible with a large item that both infants can play with at the same time, like a toy garage or a large piano. However, do not expect them to engage in this kind of play with something small and coveted, like one bucket or one shovel.

By using this strategy when there are intense conflicts over shared use of a toy, you can scaffold the infants' ability to resolve problems (see Chapter 4 for a more detailed discussion of this process). Remember, though, that many infants at this age are not aware that there is a problem or are not bothered by it, so it is rare that you will complete all the steps outlined above. Usually the adult watching the interaction feels more upset than the child.

Simply commenting that one infant is upset and wants an item often ends the conflict. It is tempting for you to take the item and hand it back to the child who was originally playing with it without explaining the problem and going through the steps of finding a solution, but this simply models bigger people taking things—the behavior that caused the problem in the first place!

**Coach children in seeing others' perspectives.** Stay close to infants who are intense and persistent, and coach all of the children about how their actions affect others. They need your help to govern their own social impulses and understand that their actions sometimes cause others to be upset. For example, you might say, "When you took the shape sorter from Lionel's hands, it made him sad. He was using it." Use the problem-solving steps outlined previously.

## Time for *Time In*

It is tempting to put a child who hits, grabs, pulls hair, or knocks down others in *time out* to think about what she did and what to do differently the next time. Older infants and young toddlers, however, can't yet reflect on what they did that was wrong, and they are still learning to regulate their impulsive responses and express strong emotions in more acceptable ways. But they *do* tell you when they need more support or personal space and less chaos in the classroom—by their behavior. It's up to you to listen.

When a child is repeatedly engaging in challenging behaviors, rather than isolate her, try engaging with her in *floor time*. Floor time is a technique created by Stanley Greenspan (1999) designed primarily to address the needs of children who are easily overwhelmed by sensory input, unable to control aggressive impulses, or experience other developmental differences, and it's an effective way for teachers and families to support children by providing *time in*.

To provide time in, find a way to spend one-on-one time with the child, focusing on her strengths and seeking connection. This special focused time works best in a calm space without other children. It seems counterintuitive to give a child more attention when she is showing challenging behavior, but when a young child is overwhelmed or needs more support from you, there aren't many ways for her to express this. The key to helping infants find a way to become calm and focused on play when they are struggling with sensory or social challenges is supporting their emotional development and sense of connection, and you can do this with special time together.

# An Engaging Environment for Mobile Infants: Safe and Inviting for Exploration

Mobile infants are quick and capable explorers, so the room design must reflect this. Since they can navigate interest areas, deciding where to be and what to do, make each place easy to access. Offer a range of choices in each area to invite infants to stretch and grow in all areas of their development. For example, mobile infants appreciate open space to push their carts and other rolling toys, but they also appreciate small hiding places and containers, such as low wicker laundry baskets, that let them to explore how their bodies fit into spaces.

When you provide a rich array of experiences that change over time and grow in complexity, you allow each infant to develop an understanding of how things work and how people engage with each other. You're dancing their dance and extending their ideas. Notice how Jazel's teacher does this:

### A 17-month-old's maturing investigations

Jazel's mother shares with Tremayne, the teacher, that at home Jazel (17 months) enjoys placing soft fabric baskets on her head as a joke. In the classroom, Tremayne adds similar baskets to build on this interest. When Jazel tries to place them on her head and can't see, Tremayne adapts, adding soft fabric hats. Delighted, Jazel starts placing the hats on her own head, her doll's head, and Tremayne's head.

Later, Tremayne notices Jazel pulling at the doll's diaper. Extending this, he sets up a doll diapering station with wipe boxes full of fabric, Velcro diapers, and a doll on a mat. Jazel begins acting out some of the steps of her own diaper change, such as placing the doll on the table and wiping the doll.

Here are some suggestions to guide your decisions around materials and room design.

## Provide Options for Children to Investigate Their Interests

Select toys that invite mobile infants to do "research" into each discovery and help them make sense of how objects work. Observe each infant and think about the skills or concepts she seems to be investigating and provide a few different options for her to explore that skill. This lets her choose to explore whatever interests her. Some examples are listed in "Choosing Materials to Support Concepts and Skills."

## Choosing Materials to Support Concepts and Skills

| If the infant is exploring the concept of . . . | Provide these types of items |
| --- | --- |
| Spatial relationships | A bin filled with birdseed or water and measuring cups to fill and dump<br><br>Boxes or yogurt containers with scarves or other fabric for infants to fill and dump |
| Object permanence or explicit memory (understanding that objects continue to exist when out of sight) | Hanging scarves or curtains for peekaboo games<br><br>A ball drop to track an object in motion and observe change<br><br>A shoebox with a lid for peering at the things inside<br><br>A large cardboard box with a door cut into it to hide inside and peek out |
| Problem solving with tools | Shovels and buckets<br><br>Spoons to practice with in the dramatic play area<br><br>Musical instruments in the music area<br><br>Hammers and ball boxes in the cognitive area (cardboard boxes with holes cut into them that match the size of the balls in your classroom; cover the boxes with contact paper or packing tape to make them easier to wash) |
| Cause and effect | Balls to toss and foam ramps to roll the balls down<br><br>Pop-up toys in which an animal pops up when a button is pushed<br><br>Wheeled carts that roll when pushed |

# Balance Familiarity with New, Intriguing Materials

While mobile infants need novelty more than they did when younger, continue to maintain a balance between too little and too much change in the materials and experiences you offer. As with younger infants, too little change can lead to mobile infants being bored because activities are too easy or too familiar. Changing items too often or too soon can cause stress or frustration for infants because the experiences are too complex to be mastered.

It is fairly easy to tell if you are not changing the materials often enough. Infants may ignore entire areas of the room, seek out the few novel items, and have conflicts over them. They may even try to open the classroom door to leave! Too much change might be indicated by differences in the children's behavior as well. Children who are slow to explore something new may camp out on your lap, unwilling to investigate. Children may become anxious if certain toys or books they used for support or a particular activity they were invested in is removed. They might express this by throwing objects or pushing other children.

**Add elements of surprise.** Use each infant's preferences to choose which materials to add and which to replace and when. Research suggests that 11-month-old infants focus more and therefore learn more when objects behave in unexpected ways rather than in ways that are predictable (Stahl & Feigenson 2015). So when you are planning experiences and arranging the environment for mobile infants, change things a little each week by adding a small surprise or something new in each interest area. This keeps them engaged in making new discoveries.

**Build on what children know.** When you are deciding to add an element of surprise, consider what the infants know and what they expect. So, for example, if infants already are familiar with what happens when cardboard blocks fall from a stack, provide a stack of fabric blocks with bells inside, adding an element of surprise as the stack jingles while falling. If infants have had lots of experiences playing in water and with paint and have come to expect that water will flow and paint will stick, put oobleck (cornstarch and water) in the sensory table. This material neither sticks nor pours but invites infants to figure out how it behaves.

**Consider what to keep the same.** Keep the interest areas predictably located (see "Interest Areas for Mobile Infants" on pages 66–69), and continue to feature materials and activities the infants are still actively engaging with. For example, change the type or size of the plastic animals so that they are different from the ones available the previous week, but keep the animals in the same location.

**Add materials in response to infants' cues.** Listening to and observing infants' cues and then making a small change to reflect their "request" is a respectful way to provide learning experiences. If you are using a camera to document the children's learning and an infant tries to take the camera, your curriculum the next week might include toy cameras for play. If infants spend time pulling at your necklace or eyeglasses, you might add sunglasses and teething beads to the dramatic play area.

This idea applies to other interests you notice as well. If the infants enjoy looking through the sunglasses (so dark!), add blocks with colorful transparent centers to extend the concept of looking through something to view the world differently. If you notice that the infants carry the pots and pans to the water table where ducks are floating, add containers to the water table to extend their interest in experimenting with containers and volume.

## Provide Several of the Same Toy

When designing spaces in the classroom, set yourself and the children up for success by providing identical multiples of toys. Infants who are imitating the actions of others and are engaging in parallel play can then expand those skills without unnecessary conflicts over sharing. If there is just one drum, for example, one infant will bang it, and another will come over to imitate the banging—and then probably try to take the drum. But if there are two identical drums on the shelf, each child is likely to select one, look at the other child, and begin to drum side by side. Problem solved!

## Provide Props for Pretend Play and Self-Help Skills

Mobile infants relish opportunities to do real-life activities themselves, like dressing up, diapering dolls, and cooking pretend food in the dramatic play area. This kind of symbolic play helps them practice fine motor skills and rehearse the steps of routines so that they can assist with elements of their own diaper changing or hand washing. The care area, though generally not considered a part of the curriculum or a place to play, is a good place to refine these skills that infants have begun to explore through play. Observation leads to better imitation.

As mobile infants refine their imitation skills, you will see them engaging in more dramatic (symbolic) play. Invite children to imitate their families at work and play by providing real-looking props such as cameras, phones, and pots and pans. Here are some suggestions for props and what infants gain from using them:

> Using real clothing and accessories (including boots, sunglasses, hats, and bags) in a play setting expands infants' self-help skills. They can practice with no pressure to dress themselves perfectly.

> Playing with real nonworking keyboards, cameras, and other technology invites infants to imitate adult roles with materials that are often not accessible at home. Real-looking dummy cell phones are particularly exciting to infants and are inexpensive.

> Medical equipment such as stethoscopes, knee hammers, and syringes (without needles) can help decrease children's fears of the medical setting and equipment. Becoming familiar with the items and being in control of using them makes the items less mysterious and intimidating. (See related vignettes on pages 84 and 120.)

Nonworking technology items should be cleaned after they are mouthed. To prevent the inner workings from rusting, clean the items with a sanitizing spray (following your setting's cleaning and sanitizing protocol) as you would a soiled book or wooden toy.

## Interest Areas for Mobile Infants

As infants approach toddlerhood, introduce more complex materials and activities. Most infants are less likely to mouth, handle, bang, and shake the materials and more likely to engage in play as adults think of it, using the same materials as tools and testing out their functions through basic problem solving.

With this in mind, invite infants into the following areas to explore more complex materials and actions.

**Gross motor area.** Make sure that there is a lot of room for mobile infants to move in your classroom. Consider adding stairs, slides, large blocks, or an obstacle course to keep them busily moving and help them refine their balance. Adapting this area every two weeks or so is helpful—active infants who are focused get into fewer conflicts. Expect children of this age to be interested in throwing things, and offer acceptable choices like soft balls and large containers to aim them at.

Place low ramps for infants to crawl up and down and a central tunnel to crawl through—high enough to pull to stand on and exciting to use for games of peekaboo. Crawling infants will enjoy moving up and down the ramp on their bellies, while walking infants will enjoy the challenge of balancing up and down the ramps.

**Art and sensory area.** Use a wider range of supplies than for younger infants, like crayons, paintbrushes, chalk, playdough tools, and easel paints (Schwarz & Luckenbill 2012). Put out enough materials to go around—for example, four to six paintbrushes or egg crayons on the table for a group of 10 infants. Remember that if an infant mouths an item, it is "his" and must be washed after he's done with it. Keep backup resources handy!

**Nature and science area.** Consider extending this area to your art and sensory space. For example, water tables with sand and water that model the habitat of a fish are exciting; infants enjoy using tools to poke at the wet sand and using their hands to catch plastic fish. Invite brand-new discoveries by adding tools or a sand mill to a bin of birdseed.

## Types of Homemade Playdough

You can make playdough very cheaply and introduce it once the children in your room are not putting items in their mouths as often. Cooked playdough lasts the longest and is resistant to mold. There are many recipes on the internet for both cooked and uncooked playdoughs. Try some that include different textures.

If you add cocoa powder, vanilla, cinnamon, or other foods with pleasant scents to your playdough, infants will most likely want to taste it. Discourage them from mouthing playdough that is too salty, and ensure that enough teachers are supervising the infants to quickly remove mouthed playdough or to prevent two infants from mouthing the same piece of playdough.

There are commercially available and recipes for making edible playdoughs that have less salt content, but most are sugar based, which some families may prefer to avoid. Avoid peanut butter and honey-based recipes for allergy reasons.

You can find wonderful playdough tools in secondhand shops. Tools such as tortilla presses and cookie cutters make strong home-to-school connections and are usually inexpensive. Sticks, twigs, pinecones, feathers, and other free natural materials also make great playdough props. Think creatively and invite mobile infants to drive toy cars and march plastic dinosaurs through the playdough.

**Cognitive area.** Feature toys that require more planning and problem solving, such as gears that fit onto boards, pegboards with pegs that fit in their holes, Primo blocks that can be pressed together if the holes and bumps line up, and ball drops into which only certain sizes of balls will fit. This area can feature building blocks like WEDGiTS, which can be linked, stacked, nested, and wedged together, or toys for exploring volume, such as stacking cups. Infants enjoy linking items such as plastic snowflake building blocks. They also love making faces at themselves in mirrored items.

**Block area.** Provide plenty of blocks, as children at this age may actually stack them. Make sure there are multiples of accessories, too, like cars or plastic people and animals, so infants can play side by side without battling for possession. Use a range of sizes, colors, and textures of both blocks and props.

**Quiet area.** Stock this area with books that contain the lyrics to songs, as infants enjoy selecting a book and bringing it to a teacher to initiate playful singing. Puppets also invite playful interactions; at this age, some infants can put on their own rigid finger puppets.

**Music area.** Have two to three of each instrument available in this area. Other children may arrive in groups, drawn by the music another child is making; each child may want to play an instrument to imitate a peer.

**Dramatic play area.** Include objects that infants can combine and take apart, such as diapers to pull off dolls and accessories infants can put on their own hands and feet. Props that encourage children to act out daily routines with dolls, such as diapering and bath time, invite them to express what they understand about these times of day through play (Greenspan 2011). Consider that during symbolic play, children imitate what they see at home, so when you provide toys such as practice chopsticks for children whose families use chopsticks, you help children make better home–school connections. This type of play is fun to scaffold by playing along with your own props.

---

Many people consider this age of infancy to be golden. You may too. Mobile infants are old enough to explore, comment, consider, and imitate, but they rarely get into serious conflict or rebellion. They adore having a play expert (you!) at their side, joining them in the fun of discovering their world.

# Where to Find More:
## Resources for Teachers and Families

"12 Types of Play Infographic": www.famlii.com/12-types-of-play-infographic

"Age-Appropriate Speech and Hearing Milestones": www.hopkinsmedicine.org/health/conditions-and
-diseases/hearing-loss/ageappropriate-speech-and-hearing-milestones

"BabySigns": www.babysignstoo.com

"Language Development: Speech Milestones for Babies": www.mayoclinic.org/healthy-lifestyle/infant
-and-toddler-health/in-depth/language-development/art-20045163?pg=2

"Making the Right Choice Simple: Selecting Materials for Infants and Toddlers," by A.N. Shabazian and C.L. Soga (*Young Children,* Vol. 69, No. 3, pp. 60–65, July 2014).

# 4

# The Toddler:
## 16 to 36 Months

Taking into account toddlers' newfound skills and interests, you must arrange the physical space and design experiences to accommodate new safety and behavior challenges—and new accomplishments! Provide gradual and intentional change based on your observations of toddlers' interests and milestones to keep them exploring and learning.

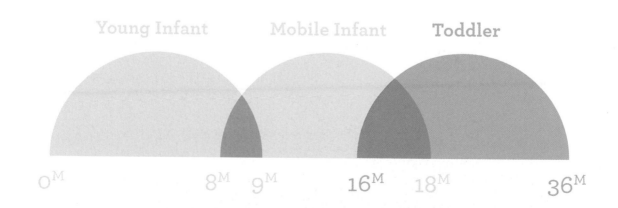

Young Infant     Mobile Infant     **Toddler**

0<sup>M</sup>     8<sup>M</sup>  9<sup>M</sup>     16<sup>M</sup>  18<sup>M</sup>     36<sup>M</sup>

# What's a Toddler Like at 16 to 24 Months?

While the toddler is still interested in imitating and observing her peers, by this time, she generally seeks possession and autonomy as a means to express herself. She may need to own all the new trucks, solve a certain puzzle, or want to carry around a specific puppet. Because she notices differences and has a greater understanding of how things work, having a particular item matters more than it used to.

This toddler may be chatty, as a language explosion typically occurs around this time. She loves to engage in imaginative play, including, for example, making noises for cows and plastic cars. She is beginning to sort out preferred objects from groups of objects, like seeking all the plastic fish. Her ability to pretend is an important skill; she expresses what she understands about the functions of objects and their understanding of social roles and events. Her play often reflects the objects and events in her household and community. Over time her ability to imitate the activities of daily living—particularly cooking, eating, cleaning, and baby care—are refined and look a lot like those in her home culture.

The young toddler is becoming more fluid in walking, running, and climbing. She grips tools in a more effective way and uses them to achieve goals like scribbling with a pen or pouring sand from a cup. In dramatic play activities, she is now more skilled at putting on slip-on boots and hats.

> *Izzy at 20 Months*
>
> Mama: What does play mean?
> Izzy: Play.
> Mama: What does it mean when you play?
> Izzy: Play.
> Mama: What does play good mean?
> Izzy: (*Strokes Mama softly.*) Play nice.
> (*Gets down to pick up her stuffed kitty, then climbs back up.*) Play with . . .

# What's a Toddler Like at 24 to 30 Months?

As she ages, the toddler develops strong opinions about ownership, routine, fashion, mealtimes, and play activities, and she will tell you all of them. She seeks out parallel play with other children using the same items and sometimes goes over to look at or take items other children are using. This leads to challenges when she wants to co-use toys with others, as her peers generally prefer to keep those items in their own hands.

This toddler may experience more difficulty than earlier when her play is interrupted or she and a playmate have different ideas about the play theme or tools to use. This is because the toddler has an idea about how she wants things to happen in play story lines but does not yet have the physical or social skills to make the idea successful or the coping skills to handle her disappointment and lack of success.

Her growing ability to follow single-step requests and commands ("Please help Rhiannon find another spoon") and greater skill with back-and-forth exchanges allow her to problem solve and participate in resolving conflict and play. Another exciting linguistic development is that you can ask this toddler what she would like to play with and get an answer! Telling you her play choices supports her planning skills and her developing ability to figure out what she likes and doesn't like.

This toddler's cognitive skills are blooming. She acts out her own stories in her play story lines and is beginning to explore the pretend world with more complexity. No longer content to simply feed her baby doll, she may invite you and the doll to a tea party and serve tea.

The toddler is also better able to complete tasks involving size and shape, such as puzzles, balls in holes, and shape sorters, especially if you are there to help when she gets stuck or distracted. She enjoys collecting items that are similar to each other, such as all the red crayons and pastels in the art area.

With the toddler's increased control of her grasp, stronger balance, and increased hand-eye coordination, she is trying new things with more skill each day, like stacking towers of large blocks and throwing balls. She can draw with both hands at the same time and on all kinds of surfaces. She may unscrew the jars in the dramatic play area and put on the pants of a costume. She can run, jump, climb, and take risks, and she wants you to see all of it.

# What's a Toddler Like at 30 to 36 Months?

As the toddler continues to develop, her play includes elements of make-believe, with invisible rabbits, big bad wolves, and imaginary witches in the bushes. With coaching, she can join a group of children engaged in an activity like shoveling sand or hide and seek. She may have one or two preferred playmates ("best friends") that she joins each day for a shared game that may involve taking turns.

She is now more willing to let her peers share or have some materials, although she sometimes keeps her favorites to herself. This means that the number of conflicts over play objects in the classroom decreases, although there are conflicts over whose idea is being played out.

She loves being helpful and usually takes you up on an invitation to help you or another toddler who is having a play challenge. She often comes to the aid of a child who asks for more tape or another block, and you find that your help is not needed as often.

She has more physical capabilities than she did a few months ago, making self-help and motor skills like getting costumes on and cleaning up after art experiments less frustrating. In the art area you see her cutting paper, gluing, making drawings that begin to look like real objects (for example, a circle on a line for a flower), and making "pizza" and "balls" in the playdough area. On the playground, she competently climbs ladders up to slides, turns around, and slides down.

This toddler often asks you to tell her stories and sing songs and sometimes even comes up with alternative endings or plays with the language in the stories. She understands two-part commands, requests, and concepts, which allows her to join in circle time activities and group movement games that involve following directions, such as freeze. She also asks many, many questions as she is figuring out logical connections between things (Zero to Three 2016). For this reason, you find yourself challenged to become very good at answering!

Toddlers are great fun. They're developing more interests and skills, becoming aware of themselves as separate beings, and engaging more in social play. Their new competencies allow you to have a more fun and active role. Following along with a child's imagination is exciting and far more complex than watching her shake a rattle not so many months ago. Now a block can be a phone, and you may be asked to call the zoo— what a development!

As is clear from the profiles above, though, toddlers keep you on your toes with their active, engaging, and social play. A large part of your role is to help them navigate their way through their interactions with each other and the challenges presented by more complex materials and experiences.

## What's a Teacher of Toddlers Like?

You adapt easily and adjust your technique depending on each toddler's temperament, keeping in mind that toddlers are less capable when they are tired, ill, or hungry. You speed up when they want to dash off to see creatures in their yard, then slow down to examine the spots on the ladybugs. You enthusiastically sing about speckled frogs jumping while the toddlers jump, then shift to a calm story about napping, lowering the play energy so children can relax. You try to stay a step ahead of social drama, noting children's preferred activities and playthings and keeping extras on hand, and you are right there to assist when you notice play going awry. Whew! You are never bored in this classroom!

# The Teacher's Role:
## Engage Children in New Experiences and Help Them Navigate Interactions

While not all children at this age are fully exploring challenging toddler behaviors—swiping toys, hitting, throwing hard objects, trumpeting "No!" and "Mine!"—some are. Although toddlers may understand that they are not supposed to do something, they are working on controlling their impulses, so conflict and tantrums may now disrupt what used to be peaceful play. You need to be prepared to help them resolve problems so they can resume their play and exploration. Many of the suggestions in this section focus on strategies for doing just that. Supporting toddlers' exploration and development is addressed in the section "An Engaging Environment for Toddlers: More Complex Opportunities for Investigating and Interacting."

### Be Aware of Both Individual Needs and Group Safety

When you're leading a classroom of toddlers who are new to parallel play and learning to see things from another's view, it can be difficult to keep track of everything that's going on in the room. Where do you place yourself to support the play of so many children? How do you both zoom in to one child's individual play needs and out to the needs of the group?

Here are some tips:

> Observe the classroom dynamics, particularly between those children who differ in their general outlook or approach to situations. They are more likely to have play challenges when they interact with each other. Be ready to step in when these children begin to play.

> Once children who need more play coaching are playing by themselves or engaged in a group activity like listening to a book, check in with the children who need less play coaching.

> Be especially alert when things are too loud or too quiet for you to track the social dynamics of the class and how they shift throughout the day. This is when it can be easy to miss something that's happening.

For example, Daya (24 months) is usually content to stay in a spot on the floor where she enjoys diapering a doll. Her care group (the children with whom she shares a teacher) also includes Lily (24 months) and Sierra (25 months). These two toddlers are much more reactive and active than Daya, flitting around the room from the dramatic play area to the climber and then to the shape sorters.

When playing with these three toddlers, you must adapt, staying close when Lily interacts with anyone, as she tends to impulsively take toys from other children—especially Sierra—rather than find more. If you know that Sierra can adapt to the typical interactions with most of the children in the room but that her response to Lily's frequent toy taking is intense and will probably lead to a tantrum, you can stay closer when you see that play story line brewing.

Since you are responsible for all three children, you can give Lily *time in* and social coaching during peer interactions, stressing that "That toy is in Sierra's hands, so let's find another one." When Lily is engaged in solo play such as art, you can check in with Daya, listening to her talk about her doll play and inviting her to try other activities such as those at the art table, and possibly joining in with Sierra or Lily.

You know that Sierra will frequently seek you out and will be involved in many social interactions with Lily, so you don't worry as much about giving Sierra a special check-in. You should, though, make a point to personalize each diaper change or toileting attempt so that each child gets at least one individual interaction a day.

This kind of social dynamic is even more complex when you look beyond this one primary care group and zoom out to consider the entire class. While your focus is primarily on children who might have more social challenges, like Lily, and on supporting children who may be slow to approach new situations, you must not forget about the children who are more flexible and need to feel like important, valued, and heard members of the community.

## Use Sportscasting to Encourage Social Play

To successfully facilitate play among toddlers, you must be soothing, patient, playful, and very capable at sportscasting and adapting: "It looks like you are climbing very close to Lita," "Deron looks worried when you get so close to his zoo. He is working hard to make the cages," or "You need to be gentle, Ella." This technique cues children about others' perspectives and allows you to set limits when needed.

## Practice Watch-Ask-Adapt

Along with sportscasting, practice the art of watch-ask-adapt, a model recommended by the Program for Infant and Toddler Caregivers (Lally et al. 1990). When working with very young children, it is tempting to step in and fix a situation, but it's wise to engage in a moment of objective reflection first. This helps you tune in to important story line cues and avoid jumping to conclusions about the play and children's actions and motivations.

Let's look at how this strategy might be used with Cate (24 months) and Zoe (26 months). You notice Cate taking several stacking cups that Zoe is playing with.

**Watch.** First, try to understand the plan or unmet need of each toddler involved. Take into consideration factors like out-of-class interactions between them, prior in-class interactions, and the children's preferences and physical and emotional states. For example, Cate has arrived tired because her new baby brother cries at night, and all her preferred comfort objects are packed in boxes for the family's move to their new home. Zoe has three older brothers and is often asked to share things. Having this type of information will help you during the ask stage.

**Ask.** Next, ask yourself, "What is going on here?" While it may appear that Cate is simply taking toys from Zoe, consider factors that may be contributing to this behavior. You know that Cate usually plays calmly by herself, and now she is suddenly swiping toys from Zoe (who also usually plays calmly by herself). You remember that Cate has a new baby at home and is moving from her familiar house to someplace she doesn't know, and you reflect that she may need more attention today—taking toys is one way to get it. Or she may want to possess more things right now since so many of her own things, her family role, and her home are being taken away.

There is also the immediate event in question: Is Zoe really upset that Cate is taking her stacking cups? Could they use the second set together? Neither toddler engages in parallel play, so perhaps this is a play bid with two unskilled co-players rather than the start of a conflict. Quickly asking yourself about all of these possible factors will prepare you to move on to the final step.

**Adapt.** Generally if you notice a problem, you move closer and use sportscasting to comment on what you see. Sometimes this support and commenting are enough. Other times you may step in, either in a minor way—for example, sitting between or behind the children in order to narrate—or by offering more resources, such as another set of cups in this case. When there is real emotion and conflict, you might decide to use conflict resolution steps (described on page 82) to help the toddlers work through the problem, but often the watch-ask-adapt process is all that's needed.

This Is Play

## Use Positive Redirection

You must set positive limits and offer redirection when social skills are still developing. Classroom social rules for toddlers should be very simple. You might ask children to be gentle with each other, be gentle with the toys, and follow safety rules. When you set limits for toddlers using these rules, say them in a positive way:

"You can touch her gently."

"You can throw soft things."

"We sit when we eat."

"You can climb on the climber."

"You can tear paper, but we touch books gently."

"That hurts! You can bite on the teether."

While it's often easier to say "No hitting" or "No throwing" than to state what you want children to do, like "Touch gently" or "Sand stays down low," negative limits are harder for toddlers to understand and follow. Also, when you overuse the word *no*, children become so used to hearing it that it ceases to have the power to stop real problems when needed. Sometimes even positive phrases can become rote and meaningless if, for example, you simply aim them in a child's direction as you're busy doing something else. Take the time to address individual children, with respect, when you remind them to touch gently or sit when they are eating.

With several little ones all around the same developmental age in a classroom, drama can ensue quickly. However, if you are consistent about the classroom social rules, such as items remaining in someone's hands while they are in use, most toddlers will grow in their ability to show care toward each other.

## Help Toddlers Choose a Different Way

It may seem that toddlers are always in conflict, and it is tempting to think to yourself that they should just share or leave each other alone. But their social skills are still developing, and they need you to support them with specific strategies. Stepping in and out of a play situation with gentle tips, perspectives, and reframing statements can help toddlers get along far better in play that you might anticipate.

For example, you might be setting up snack and notice two toddlers stacking blocks next to each other. You see a third toddler walking over who you know enjoys knocking things down. It is easy enough to take a moment to observe the play and comment to the third child that the play happening in that area is building, and that more blocks for knocking down are in a different location. This takes very little time, and the stacking play can continue for longer.

But if you ignore this potential play conflict and don't provide the third child a cue about finding different blocks to play with, you may need to stop your snack setup entirely to handle the screaming and kicking that occur after the block stacking ends with a crash and two angry block stackers take matters into their own hands.

Toddlers have limited executive function skills—like self-control, working memory, and mental flexibility—so controlling the impulse to take a friend's toy, waiting for snack when they are hungry, remembering the story line you're sharing in a book, or sustaining and shifting their attention are very hard tasks, if not impossible. Children need your support to resist impulses and choose a different course of action.

## Be Mindful of Your Own Buttons

Understand your own hot spots—things children do or say that upset you (Brault & Brault 2005). You should know, for example, if biting or hitting or defying adults causes you to become angry at a toddler. Work to check your emotions and change your response when the behavior occurs. Know what your coteachers' hot spots are too.

Understanding why you tend to respond as you do and learning more supportive techniques will help you avoid using negative labels—even to yourself—like *bully, crybaby,* or *biter* for those toddlers who are less skilled at interactions and controlling their impulses than others. The resources section at the end of this chapter lists some tools, such as the BRAULT Behavior Checklist, to help you identify which child behaviors particularly upset you and learn strategies for responding effectively.

## Analyze the Routines and Classroom for Clues to Behavior

If challenging behaviors crop up a lot, look closely at the program design or routines to determine if they are playing a role in the toddlers' behaviors. While biting, hitting, and resisting are typical behaviors among many toddlers, it is still likely that the setting is contributing to difficulties in managing emotions and behavior. If you can identify what that is and change it, fewer challenges will occur. Here are a few common examples.

If you notice these behaviors:

> Biting occurs while toddlers wait for everyone to put on shoes to go outside.
> Several toddlers regularly and loudly insist that the one blue fish puppet is "mine!" Other puppets go unused, and no purposeful play is occurring.
> A toddler pushes others when he is crowded by other children or at the top of the climber.

Try making these adjustments:

> Have children go outside one group and teacher at a time, decreasing wait time and crowding at the door.
> Remove the coveted fish puppet or find several identical blue fish.

> ❯ Observe the toddler who is pushing. Could he feel trapped because he can't get out of the loft or down the slide or steps? Maybe his pushing is his way of communicating his discomfort with this lack of space. Try limiting the number of toddlers in an area or help this child find a less crowded space where he won't feel trapped.

If you objectively examine your schedule, room setup, and the experiences you provide, you may find that making changes to one or more of those elements leads to a dramatic decrease in challenging behavior. For example, too many demands for sharing may lead to children taking toys from each other rather than finding other options.

## What About Sharing?

Toddlers are not developmentally equipped to share, but they are able to take turns. It may be tempting during the many toddler conflicts in a given day for you to demand that children share, immediately, thinking this will help them learn to get along and be nice to each other. But think about whether you would follow such a demand yourself. If you were using your cell phone and someone else insisted she use it, you might say no or tell her it's okay to use it when you are done, but you would not hand it over right then (Shumaker 2012). Instead of insisting that toddlers share, guide them to use the phrase "You can use it when I'm done." This invites generosity and also allows toddlers, who are working on becoming independent people who can exert some control over a situation, to stay in charge of preferred possessions.

## Consider Varying Needs for Sensory Information

Some children require a lot of sensory information or stimulation from the environment in order to connect and interact (Williamson & Anzalone 2001). A toddler may not respond to play bids and playful interactions unless the other person uses obvious signals—a wide smile, big gestures, and a very bright tone. She may seek out interaction by using deep hugs, lots of touching, mouthing, pushing, and similar behaviors. This can be a challenge in play, as she can be unintentionally rough with co-players and may not understand when others tell her not to play in that way.

Other children appear easily overwhelmed by information they take in through their senses. They may try to avoid things that overwhelm them, such as loud toys, loud playmates, and crowded areas of the classroom.

Having toddlers with varying reactions to sensory information can lead to social conflicts in play and make it challenging for you to supervise them and scaffold their play attempts. Use activities they have in common, such as squeezing and poking playdough or reading books together, to help them adapt to others who have different needs and preferences.

## Use Toddlers' Helpfulness to Advantage

You can alleviate high emotions simply by tuning in, offering support and feedback, and allowing the toddler some control in the classroom. For example, he can help sweep up spilled birdseed—a fun activity with a toddler-size broom!—as a gentle redirect from dumping it or from the frustration of being crowded at the birdseed table or having a preferred cup taken over by another toddler.

You will find that if you are playful, many toddlers are good helpers when play goes wrong. A toddler can help you find tape for a torn book, clean up paint that she added to the table, and find a cold teether after a block falls on her stacking playmate. The more opportunities she has to become a member of the community and be part of the plan during playtime, the more likely she is to go along with adult-led activities and transitions when needed and to see herself as part of a community of helpers.

## Support Problem Solving

To address a social conflict in the moment, you can use a simplified version of HighScope's conflict resolution process developed for slightly older children (Evans 2016). While preschoolers can eventually use this process themselves to work through conflicts with each other, toddlers rely heavily on you to facilitate the process. Success also depends on the communication skills of the children involved and on how overwhelmed they are in the moment.

Here are the basic steps for working through a conflict between children (Evans 2016, 23–30):

1. Approach calmly, stopping any hurtful actions.
2. Acknowledge children's feelings.
3. Gather information.
4. Restate the problem.
5. Ask for ideas for solutions and choose one together.
6. Be prepared to give follow-up support.

It helps to co-hold an object with the children involved if it is causing the conflict. This neutralizes it by preventing tugging and obscuring it from the toddlers' sight. Co-holding while stopping the hurtful actions allows children to focus on the conversation rather than on retaining possession of the item. You may feel tempted to hold the toy by yourself, but this models to toddlers that bigger people take things, which is less than ideal. Toddlers don't understand justice in the same way older children do. If you do need to take the item, explain why: "I'm going to hold this for both of you while we talk about the problem."

When toddlers are in conflict, emotions run high and they are not able to participate in the calm reasoning required for problem solving. It's important that you help a child regain calm first and then help him solve the problem. You may need to provide physical comfort, such as holding the child or rubbing his back while speaking in a quiet, soothing tone about his strong feelings. Then you can help the toddlers involved find a solution everyone can live with.

Young toddlers rarely get beyond the second or third step of conflict resolution, but that's okay. When a child walks away or gives the toy back, simply jump to the last step: "It looks like we solved the problem! Joaquin doesn't want the bus anymore, and you can have it, Amelie," or "It looks like he didn't know you wanted the bus, and now he gave it to you." Don't try to continue the steps just for the sake of completing all of them.

Older toddlers might participate a little more in the process:

### Resolving a conflict with 28-month-olds

| | | |
|---|---|---|
| Teacher: | Desmond, I hear you saying that you want the ball, and Gerry took it. That makes you upset. I wonder what we can do. | |
| Desmond: | Mine. | |
| Teacher: | You think the ball is yours, and Gerry took it. Maybe we can find another ball that is the same. | |
| Desmond: | No. | |
| Teacher: | Well, let's get another ball and see if Gerry will trade it. Gerry, when you took the ball from Desmond's hands, it made him upset. Can you give him that ball and use this one instead? | |
| Gerry: | Yeah. | |
| Teacher: | It looks like we solved the problem. Now you both have a ball and you both look happy. I wonder if you will roll the balls or kick them. | |

## Revisit Conflicts Together

If you coach toddlers while everyone is calm, often they learn more. If you wait until children are already upset to step in and support them, you may find that reasoning with them is not effective. They often cannot engage in two-way communication until they can regulate their intense feelings and reconnect with a hug or a cuddle. You can revisit the challenge after the storm is over, but the participants may have walked away or even forgotten what the social drama was about altogether!

This said, if you miss the moment of brewing drama because you were elsewhere, all is not lost. When you stay calm and focus on helping toddlers calm themselves, they can regain composure and then you can revisit the upsetting event, talking about what might have been done, the feelings, and what might be done next time the social challenge occurs again in a play episode (Da Ros & Kovach 1998).

Over time this guidance will lead to positive social skill development. Since older toddlers can understand right from wrong (Vaish, Carpenter, & Tomasello 2016), patiently and consistently coaching them in social situations is quite effective, much more so than when they were younger. You might say to a child, "I could see that you were really upset when Aliah offered you sand cake in her bucket and then ran off with it. But scratching hurts. Next time, you can ask a teacher for help or you can use your words. Or you could make another sand cake in your bucket."

## What Does a Successful Play Episode with Toddlers Look Like?

Many toddlers are not yet ready to sustain play in a group, but with skillful coaching and suggestions, you can help them begin to engage together.

### Scaffolding a play episode with older toddlers

Cami (30 months), Liza (29 months), and Kasharee (29 months) are seated with their teacher, Nichelle, in the dramatic play area, which is outfitted as a doctor's office area. Liza is wrapping a long bandage around her arm. "I want one," Kasharee says with a slight frown, so Nichelle locates another one and comments, "Now you have a bandage, too."

Cami holds a stethoscope and looks at her teacher. "Are you feeling better?" Nichelle asks Cami and Liza. Cami shakes her head no.

"I wonder if your heart is working." Nichelle says to Cami. "Shall we use a stethoscope to find out?" Cami nods. Nichelle takes another stethoscope from the shelf and puts it on. She listens to Cami's heart. "I hear thump, thump, thump," she reports.

Cami smiles again and puts on her own stethoscope. Turning to Kasharee, she puts the end of the tool on Kasharee's chest and says, "Bump, bump, bump." Nichelle says, "Cami, you are checking to see if Kasharee is better!" Kasharee smiles at Cami.

Although these three toddlers are all interested in the same materials, each is engaged in exploring them in her own way. Teacher Nichelle encourages (but does not insist on) interaction among the children by joining the play, using interesting words such as bandage and stethoscope, and modeling a way to include a playmate by using the stethoscope (a novel tool). She also validates Cami's play bid with Kasharee and invites Kasharee to join in the play.

## Keep Play in Prosocial Territory

**Give toddlers control of their play.** When you play with older toddlers, it's easy to get carried away and lead the play instead of letting them lead. This is because toddlers can comment, imitate, laugh at adults they find entertaining, and follow directions. Keep in mind, though, that toddlers get the most from their play when they can control the direction. Building on their play cues—"You want me to sit here? And you want to feed me?"—gives them some control, and when toddlers have more control in play, they are less likely to initiate power struggles at times when they have no choices (Karp 2015).

Your goal is to support the play as it unfolds in the child's head, making suggestions within the same topic. If the child appears stuck or frustrated, or if another child wants to join in, you might take control for a moment, offering ideas that could remedy the situation: "I wonder if he can have a cookie too," or "It looks like you have too many cookies for your hand. Do you want a bowl?," or "It looks like Hazel is using all the cookies right now. I have some delicious pasta you can use instead if you want." Using phrases such as "I wonder" and "It looks like" allows you to join and shape the play rather than direct it. This also models problem solving for the toddlers.

**Use humor.** Using humor and play as a tool to support children at this age is vital. For example, if toddlers are starting to say no to each other—perhaps one toddler is trying to join the play and the other is upset at the intrusion—you can repeatedly sing "No" to the tune of "Shake Your Sillies Out" until you get to the end and then sing "Yes!" This is a humorous redirect to get toddlers playing together again. Or, if you have two toddlers who both want to be at the top of the climber because it is the fire station and both want to use the large attached hose, you can unite them in a goal to save you: "Oh, no, there's a fire, firefighters! Can you use the hose together and put out the fire? That hose is so big and heavy!" As you coach them to work together with a shared goal, they both feel powerful as they save you, and this shifts them from seeking power by owning the top of the climber.

## Be Okay with Repetition

The older toddler enjoys inviting you to join in repetitive dramatic play ("Ask the babies who wants cookies!") and may assign roles to you and willing peers. When you follow her lead, you might offer props that could extend the play: "The gears are cookies?" But avoid taking over the story line by demanding "Make cookies for me," for example. You might ask which baby needs a cookie or if they might also like milk, still leaving the toddler in control of the story. You might be tempted to change the subject or the game because *you* are bored ("Oh, this baby needs a diaper change"), but avoid this temptation. Repetition is how toddlers learn.

## Know When to Step Back and Step In

As toddlers develop, they add more tools to their toolkits. With older toddlers, you can step back a bit during playtime to let them try their own skills at practicing self-care tasks, taking on physical challenges, and managing conflicts. This may be slow and messy, but it's worth the effort. With support and practice, older toddlers can sometimes work out solutions to their own social, physical, and self-care problems without you.

If not, especially in moments when social dramas escalate during play, be ready to step in, help each child understand the needs and perspective of the other, stay with the children until a solution is reached, and make sure the solution is mutually acceptable. Compared with when they were younger, older toddlers may quickly and easily come up with their own possible solutions to the problem and may only need your help in remaining calm, listening to each other's ideas, and perhaps locating materials for follow-through.

## Begin Using the Language of Planning

Introduce planning to older toddlers. For example, ask a child, "What do you plan to play after snack? . . . Oh, the sand mill in the sandbox?" Follow up with him at the end of playtime: "Did you end up using the sand mill?" The act of planning what to do, doing it, and then revisiting what they did can help children find meaning in their experiences and be more deliberate about the things they choose to do. This process also strengthens a variety of cognitive skills that will be helpful to children as they work and play more and more independently.

## Introduce a Few Adult-Led Activities

You may wish to add a few adult-led activities to the many open-ended play activities you provide. Most older toddlers can participate in short group music and movement activities, such as using simple rhythm instruments or playing active movement and dancing games like ring-around-the-rosy, parachute, freeze, and Bluebird Through My Window. You can also invite them to join in simple cooking projects, help you plant and harvest vegetables, and feed class pets.

You are likely to find that toddlers enjoy revisiting these adult-modeled activities themselves during playtime. Provide time and materials for toddlers to

> Re-enact songs and stories on flannel boards that you have done with the group
> Retell puppet stories with simple plots
> Revisit food prep activities like making juice in the dramatic play area
> Continue gardening activities, such as watering, when they are outdoors

## Be a Ringleader to Enhance Toddlers' Play Together

As toddlers begin to play together more and more, you can become a ringleader for their play. When you notice children being able to make a group goal and join in imaginary play, listen for opportunities to invite them into play together. If a toddler says, "I'm making a train," add to and extend the play by bringing over more chairs and inviting other children to be passengers. Offer props like luggage, tickets, and hats. Help negotiate challenges, such as who will drive and whether Spider-Man can get on the train.

At this age, it is your scaffolding that brings most pretend play to life. Watch for children's play cues and expand on them. If children are pretending to push the buttons of a cash register or eat the plastic food, say, "Oh, you are selling me this banana?" or "The food at this picnic is really delicious." In this way you invite toddlers to try out new ideas and also expand their vocabulary.

When you spy a toddler hiding, invite the others to look around and find him, then animatedly model hiding your face and counting. Your self-talk guides them in the rhythms and patterns of games with rules: "I'm looking over here. Is Amad under the table? Nooo . . ." This focuses and engages the children, strengthening their ability to attend to the activity. Your support in this type of game will help expand their thinking and creativity.

## Mixed-Age Classrooms

If your class includes both infants and toddlers, consider clustering the children in mixed-age care groups—in which the age span is 9 months or so—instead of by similar age. Mixed-age groupings provide opportunities for wonderfully sensitive interactions. Here are some techniques and strategies for classroom design and supporting the interactions among children of different ages.

**Set up the classroom for success.** Provide spaces where nonmobile infants can sit and be safe and spaces for toddlers to move freely without having to try to avoid the infants.

**Set clear, short, positive limits.** Limit class rules to three simple rules. You might choose these:

1.  We are gentle with each other.
2.  We are safe.
3.  We use our toys gently.

When children hurt each other, engage in unsafe behaviors, or break toys, tell them what *to* do. Model or coach the replacement behavior: "You can sit while you eat" or "I can help you."

**Provide developmentally appropriate challenges.** Give nonmobile infants treasure baskets or a few toys set on a blanket nearby. For toddlers, design interest areas with choices that are rotated over time, becoming more complex as the toddlers master new skills.

**Support play and interactions.** Older toddlers in the group are generally the play leaders. They can engage in imaginary play and describe their ideas, which often come from books that they enjoy. Add props that can be used for more basic symbolic play (diapering, feeding, pretending to cook) that younger infants prefer. If the older toddlers are engaged as a group in dramatic play themes, younger toddlers often join in, even if they do not yet play this way at home. Because it is so exciting to make "magic potions," "go on an airplane," or "hunt sharks" with the older toddlers, most of the group will join in!

Older toddlers often continue to consider the younger ones as their "babies" and may exclude them from their play. Here are a couple of ways to address this:

>   Encourage and provide support for younger and older children to play together but do not insist on it.

>   Respect the wishes of older children to have their own play, and join a younger child in playing alongside the group.

Note how this teacher supports both the older and younger children in her care group:

## Negotiating play involvement with toddlers of different ages

Elissa (34 months) turns to Yinjou (26 months), who is following her into the playhouse in the yard. "You can't play here," she says. "Only me and Holly can play here. This is where we make potions for the witch." Yinjou frowns. She does not say anything, but she does not move.

Their teacher says to Yinjou, "It looks like Elissa and Holly are making potions. I think they are using the bottles and the sand here." Then she asks Elissa and Holly, "I wonder, could Yinjou be the witch or help get ingredients for the potion?"

At this age, group play is fragile, and adding a third player who is less skilled can end a play episode. So the teacher is scaffolding, encouraging the older girls to include Yinjou without demanding it and suggesting a way Yinjou could be involved. By making this suggestion, the teacher offers Elissa control while respecting Yinjou's interest in joining. If Elissa says yes to the suggestion, the teacher will stay close and make sure that Yinjou understands not to dump out the potions, which would ruin the game. If Elissa says no, the teacher might offer to make potions with Yinjou in similar play nearby so Yinjou can still be part of the theme without disrupting Elissa and Holly's play.

Similar techniques can be used with children who are in different places in their intellectual, social, emotional, or physical development.

Overall, mixed-age rooms should include predictable areas with items that are safe for all the children but involve challenges that match each child's development. Active and calm areas and opportunities for children to engage in solitary, parallel, and small group play both indoors and outdoors are important elements of a good play space.

## Reinforce Options for Social Roles

Toddlers are learning a great deal about social roles from you. When you reinforce through positive interaction and validation that she is a powerful firefighter or he is a tender daddy, you send messages that grownups can take on many roles and that it is okay for children to try on whichever ones feel comfortable to them.

### Supporting a 20-month-old female firefighter

Diamond (20 months) loves to be a "firefightah." She puts on a plastic yellow hat, sits on a plastic fire truck, and scoots forward, saying, "Whee-o! Whee-o!" "Diamond, I see you're going to a fire," says her teacher, Devon. "Do you need a hose?" "Yeah!" says Diamond.

While it may be tempting to encourage girls to play with dolls in the house area and to guide boys to drive the fire truck and put out fires, Devon is committed to providing props and encouragement for all children to try various social roles. For example, she uses the term *firefighter* rather than *fireman* and encourages Diamond to pursue her chosen activity rather than try to steer her toward a stereotypical feminine activity.

## Expand Toddler Interests with Real-Life Opportunities

With the ability to follow two-part directions emerging in older toddlers, you can provide opportunities for play and real life to connect. For example, if you observe toddlers pretending to make lemonade or spaghetti in the dramatic play area, provide experiences for them to actually carry out these activities that they're imagining. Toddlers can do many tasks, including breaking up pasta, stirring, squeezing fruit, and pouring water, so these extensions of the play teach self-help and fine motor skills while capitalizing on toddler interest.

Simple field trips are another way to build on the topics of interest. Here are some examples of bringing real life and children's play together.

## Expanding on older toddlers' interests

Kamiko, Ladli, Moses, and Eva (30–32 months) are all interested in potties and in acting out the steps of potty training, though all are in different stages of the actual activity, with some fully trained. Since it is not feasible to permit the children to play for extended times in the care area, the teachers add small plastic chairs and cut out crescents from cardstock to create lids to tape to the "potties." They add two sinks with soap; create a curtain for privacy from a play storefront; and supply new underwear, toilet paper, diapers, and books about potties. The area immediately becomes busy with toddlers wanting to try the potties themselves or to put their dolls on the potties. Through this play children can explore their understanding and anxieties about the real potty and master the key steps of using it without the stress of having to produce actual results. This is important for children who are at an age where imaginary things such as being flushed down the toilet seem scary and possible.

Atticus (32 months) and Olivia (33 months) are interested in the way things move—how balls roll down ramps, how balls fall when you throw them, or what happens when toys are knocked from shelves or dropped from the climber. They also love water play inside and outside. Their teachers create a water feature from pool noodles, bamboo, rocks, and sand. Water can flow through the pool noodles via two hoses, then out into a sandy "river" edged with stones. The children can modify the water course to change both flow and the size of the pond, and they can block the flow of the river. Both children, along with their entire class, spend hours investigating the movement of the water and items in it. Teachers stay close beside them, asking "I wonder" questions to support their thinking as the toddlers test and refine their ideas.

Abinav (30 months) is passionate about trucks. He knows all the names of the trucks at the construction site that he passes on the way to the program, and he enjoys driving the yellow plastic excavators around in the block area. Imogen (30 months) and Zoe (30 months) are also interested in construction zones. Their teacher, Juan, takes the group to a nearby construction site and parks the buggy just beyond the fence. The children observe as the trucks do their heavy moving. When the children go back to the classroom, Juan adds leaves and bark as accessories to the block area so that the children will have "dirt piles" to move with their plastic trucks, similar to what they observed on their field trip.

# An Engaging Environment for Toddlers:
## More Complex Opportunities for Investigating and Interacting

Your classroom should invite action and pretend play as well as investigation of concepts and ideas that fascinate toddlers: what their bodies can do, how things work, what things look like from different viewpoints, how things fit together (and come apart), and how things change when used in different ways. These experiences expand their persistence and improve their ability to attend to an activity for longer periods of time.

Be sure to provide duplicate items for children and to design opportunities for children to interact in their play. For example, securely hang a curtain in the room to invite two children to hide behind it and peek out at you. (Try pulling on it first to make sure it is not likely to fall on children if they pull too hard, and be sure there aren't cords hanging down that could entangle children.)

### Designing the Play Space for Toddlers 16 to 24 Months

Here's a look at how you could design play areas when the children are around 16 to 24 months old.

**Gross motor and music area.** You can combine music and movement, as toddlers (and adults!) need space to dance and perform. Be sure to keep musical instruments out of the fall zone of your climber, if there is one.

Provide space and materials that allow mild risk taking, like jumping from a mattress to the ground. Other suggestions:

> Make a simple climber using two sets of low stairs back to back. Increase the challenge by placing items in between them or by adding a tunnel, slide, or large blocks.

> Provide balls in different sizes: small balls to throw (with large containers to aim at); medium-size ones to roll; and large ones to carry, push, or sit on (kickball or beach ball size, perhaps even yoga balls).

> Supply push toys: These should not be walkers, and children should access them on their own by crawling or walking, not by being placed in them. Watch children who are just beginning to walk to be sure large push toys with wheels are not too fast for the amount of force applied to them. If they roll out from under children, replace them with low chairs or even big blocks to push around. Look for push toys with a function for play—grocery carts that don't tip are fun to push and also can be filled! Be careful to purchase carts that won't tip over if a child applies lots of force to the handle.

> Purchase shakers of different sizes, weights, sounds, or colors, or make your own using empty water bottles (with the lids glued shut and then duct-taped) or food storage containers (fun to stack). Add a unique surprise, like glitter that moves when shaken, bubbles, or a ladybug bead hiding inside.

> Add drums, pianos, xylophones, rhythm sticks, marimbas, rain sticks, tambourines, or concertinas, and change them out occasionally to renew interest.

In active spaces, be sure that nonmobile children are protected from being run over by push toys!

**Quiet area.** Locate this area well away from other areas—in a corner or a loft is great. If a child misses her family, this can be a nurturing, calm, familiar place for regrouping. Consider including some of these items:

> Board books, picture books, nonfiction books

> Wordless books to invite conversation

> Books with gentle, familiar homelike rhymes, such as *Goodnight Moon*

> Books that reflect the children's languages, families, communities, and experiences

> Homemade books about the toddlers, their families, and their routines

> Comfortable pillows with soft stuffed animals

> Low bookshelves

See "Are Books Just for the Quiet Area? No!" on page 94 for ways to use books throughout the classroom.

## Are Books Just for the Quiet Area? No!

Books should be everywhere in your classroom, related to the interest areas, so that you and toddlers can learn more about topics that ignite their curiosity.

> Dramatic play area: Provide books about diverse families so that you and the toddlers can talk about family routines (such as how different people go to bed or eat meals) and activities (such as going to the park or zoo) together. Showing toddlers that people share the same needs and goals even if they do things differently is a great message for your classroom community.

> Cognitive area: Add books about colors, shapes, and sizes so children can learn the names for the objects and shapes of the toys in this area.

> Nature and science area: Include books about a variety of things found in nature so toddlers can learn where objects come from (for example, shells at the sea, sticks under trees).

> Music area: Provide books with words you can sing or chant so toddlers can sing or gesture along, sometimes to the beat or rhythm of the area's musical instruments.

> Block area: Add books about vehicles and architecture so the children can see that building and building tools are related to real life.

**Block and accessory area.** Many young toddlers are not yet focused on stacking blocks. As they become more interested in homemade blocks, it's exciting to see the cognitive and physical discoveries made in the block area carry over to other areas and activities. This is because functional play has begun. This means the toddlers can hold an idea in their heads as they play, such as the stack of blocks they will make. To support their budding construction play, offer some of these materials:

> Large blocks for toddlers interested in stacking and knocking

> Small blocks, like tree blocks made from natural tree branches, unit blocks, and cubical plastic blocks for smaller stacks and as props to use to fill plastic trucks, feed to plastic dinosaurs, and carry around

> A variety of other blocks to change out every now and then: cardboard, fabric, vinyl, homemade, and wooden blocks

> Accessories like vehicles, plastic animals and people, pieces of fabric, tubes, and ramps—these kinds of props are often more popular than the blocks themselves!

> Blocks with a transparent center for peekaboo games, purchased or made from cardboard boxes and transparent film

> Hammers and pegs

**Art and sensory area.** Toddlers' growing verbal skills mean that they can tell you their play choices. If your art area has shelving, you can provide choices such as tape, playdough, crayons, scissors, stickers, and paper. You can ask the toddler which items you should put on the table, and he can both help decide and set up the activity. These art and sensory materials work well for toddlers:

> Tools that encourage cause-and-effect exploration, like small, wide shaving brushes (easy for small hands to grip) to spread paint on butcher paper

> Crayola Pip-Squeaks markers, washable and sized for small hands: tie strings to them to keep them in the art area and to prevent choking; remove caps

> Large crayons: melt crayon bits together into larger shapes

> Large chalk: keep windows open and vacuum up any dust created

> Less messy materials like crayons and chalk can be used to create an ongoing mural on a covered wall or easel or for temporary exploration on a table or covered floor

> Baby wipes for children who avoid messy play to cope with paint on their hands; these also prevent paint from spreading as children go to the care area to wash their hands (if the areas are separate)

**Cognitive area.** Set up this area to invite exploration of key concepts.

> Problem solving and holding things in memory: toys that can involve making a plan, such as stringing large wooden beads on a pipe cleaner to create a necklace like one the child has seen someone else make

> Volume and hand-eye coordination:

  - Duplo blocks—provide enough that several toddlers can build side by side. Pushing the blocks together requires toddlers to understand the volume of the holes on the bottoms of the blocks and the bumps on the top and that pressing them together makes them stick.
  - Pegboards invite toddlers to make tall stacks, inserting each peg into the hole of another peg.
  - Cups and cylinders that nest inside each other also let toddlers explore these concepts.

> Size and shape, how things fit together: create a series of ramps with various textures affixed for toddlers to roll things down and more complex shape sorters, which you can make by cutting cardboard boxes so that they have holes that match toys you have or holes that require problem solving to use; cover the boxes with clear tape (except over the holes) to allow for easy wiping

> Using tools to hammer balls into holes in a box: make this with a cardboard box and balls that just fit the holes, and use hammers from play construction kits

With many of these toys, toddlers must keep track of the items and then find them again to repeat the game. Use sportscasting to help them focus on that process.

**Nature and science area.** Natural items invite rich exploration and discoveries. Bringing them indoors is especially beneficial when outside access is limited. Change out these items based on what's happening in nature!

> Pieces of plants, wool, or gourds
> A bowl of shells to handle, sort, and dump
> A fish tank or an insect tank for silkworms, crickets, snails, or beetles

Young toddlers enjoy observing and commenting on the insects and other invertebrates. Touch the insects gently to model respect and care for living things and to teach compassion. Children can also learn to help feed the fish, which teaches them responsibility.

**Dramatic play area.** Props in this area will invite play that looks far different from when the children were younger. For example, the toddler at this age likely understands that trains can be linked and are designed to travel along tracks, and she may even say "choo-choo" as she rolls the train along. Provide items that reflect the children's home lives and communities as well as their interests.

> Props for housekeeping and other activities of daily living, such as shopping, going to the doctor, and driving vehicles
> Diverse baby dolls, beds, high chairs, doll diapers, strollers, pretend food, and diverse hats and clothing items for dressing up like adult family members
> Homemade or purchased dolls, fabric for dressing or carrying the dolls, and bowls and spoons
> Cash registers and shopping carts
> Items from nature: stumps or nontoxic branches (these can help set the stage for a picnic just as much as a checkered fabric on the floor)
> Cardboard boxes with doors cut in them and circles traced on the side to use as trains and cars
> Props that invite the toddlers to pretend to bake cupcakes and put them into an oven, move a cow into a barn and feed it, drive a truck, or navigate trains along wooden tracks

## Materials on a Budget

Many materials for the toddler classroom can be homemade or purchased secondhand. Another way to work within a limited budget is to ask local businesses to donate props. For example, a local pizza shop may donate pizza boxes that match the cardboard pizza-shaped circles you cut out. Cutting a plain white adult T-shirt in half lengthwise creates two aprons. Paired with the flatware and dishes you already have and some uncolored playdough with rolling pins, you can make your own toddler pizza shop. You might even visit a local pizza shop to see the action and taste a sample.

**Outside play area.** Toddlers should have access to an outdoor area. Ideally, they can spend a third of their day outside. Within the constraints of your space and climate, set up a few interest areas like those indoors, although with fewer props. Toddlers don't need expensive equipment, simply inventive teachers! Look for materials like these:

> Natural elements of the yard, such as fallen leaves, wet sand, mud, flowers, shells, rocks, and plants
> Sensory materials like birdseed, sand, water, and soil
> A designated easel and art supplies or large sidewalk chalk
> A playhouse for playing peekaboo: purchase a commercial one or make one using a refrigerator box (though it will not withstand rain)—toddlers' key activities will likely be peekaboo through windows and opening and closing doors, so create multiple doors and windows to limit conflict
> Rhythm and music instruments like shakers, tubs for drums, and cymbals
> Sandbox: shovels, buckets, mills, and sifters; rotate additional props to invite dramatic play, like muffin tins, pots, cooking spoons, whisks, a small stove or table to set things on, dump trucks, and cement trucks
> Climber or a low slide or tunnel, low ramps, and rocking horses
> Kickballs

As toddlers master different ways of moving and seek new physical challenges, change out small equipment for items that can be used in more complex ways.

# Designing the Play Space for Toddlers 24 to 30 Months

As you would with younger children, design the classroom for slightly older toddlers carefully. Provide designated interest areas that are predictably located and filled with several identical developmentally appropriate toys. The difference at this point is that you can provide more challenge and more opportunities for toddlers with growing language skills and other capabilities to explore and experiment with a variety of open-ended materials.

Toddlers are always "researching" to figure things out! A toddler might spy a crumb on the floor (making an observation) and put it in her mouth to find out if it's something to eat (conducting an experiment to test out her idea about the material). If she finds that it tastes yucky (analyzing), she will probably spit it out and may even bring it to you (sharing her conclusions). Of course, the next crumb she sees *may* need to be tested in the same way—there may be a different result!

So set up interest areas and materials in ways that invite toddlers to wonder about something—What can I do with this drum and that rhythm stick? What is this stuff sticking to my hands? If I touch Roberto, will it stick to him?—and to experiment to figure out answers to their questions. Observe children carefully to understand what they're interested in, then plan experiences and materials that will help extend their explorations and their understanding.

Your intentional support of toddlers' investigations will scaffold their understanding and encourage them to make connections between what they already know and what they're observing and discovering. Use the strategies discussed throughout this book, like sportscasting and expanding on what children say, to help toddlers move from simple observations to a greater understanding of the properties of objects and what can be done with them.

Following are things to consider as you set up and change out interest areas in the toddler room to support toddlers' explorations and discoveries.

**Gross motor area.** This area is essential for toddlers, as they have an innate need to move and to refine their ability to do so (Carlson 2011). If you do not provide safe spaces and opportunities for them to develop their large motor skills, toddlers will find other ways to meet their needs, like running laps and crashing into things or climbing on shelving. If it is impossible to provide large motor challenges in your classroom but you have an easily accessible yard, consider how you might give toddlers access to both spaces at once so they can choose the outdoor space if they need to. On the other hand, if you do not have a suitable outdoor space for toddlers, the indoor gross motor area is all the more vital.

Be intentional about arranging materials and equipment in the gross motor area just as you are with other interest areas. How do you see children using their bodies? Arrange the space so toddlers can tinker with designs or concepts and innovate like they do in other areas of the room. For example, provide movable items like large foam blocks, balls, and pillows or bean bags. Open-ended designs are exciting for toddlers.

Key motor skills that toddlers are exploring at this age include alternating feet, jumping, balancing, and climbing. If you provide a set of small stairs leading to a mattress, children can alternate feet up the stairs, then jump down. On or next to the mattress you can provide other large foam shapes (covered in oilcloth) so that the toddlers can also design their own jumping challenges, like trying to balance on materials that are less firm than the wooden stairs. You will find that toddlers are quite capable of coming up with new ideas and that they know themselves fairly well; they rarely invent designs they cannot handle.

This kind of rough-and-tumble play is often discouraged in classrooms, but it is essential. You need to stay close and narrate who is jumping and when in order to keep children from crashing, but you'll know from the smiles on their faces that the play is well worth your efforts.

**Quiet area.** Encourage creative problem solving by furnishing this area with items that invite toddlers to tell their own stories. This helps toddlers connect the stories to their own lives and is a great way for them to express their emotions and ideas through play. It also invites a lot of language.

> Homemade items like emotion faces on craft sticks that are laminated for beginning puppet play

> Felt props and a felt board for reenacting circle time activities and designing stories

> A writing station with props to imitate signing in and writing letters

> Laminated cutout photos of family members, which invite storytelling about home and can be transported to other areas to enhance children's play

**Block area.** Older toddlers enjoy the challenge of stacking and creating walls, towers, and roads. They are learning spatial reasoning and spatial language as they do so (Cohen & Emmons 2017). Increase the number of blocks you provide, making sure there are plenty for many children to use at once, side by side rather than in shared efforts. It's fun to design this area to reflect the interests of the children as you see their emerging ideas hatch.

For example, if children enjoy making roads, provide props that enhance road making, such as cars, trucks, traffic signs, pedestrians, and trees. Recycled materials like bubble wrap or sandpaper could be used to represent elements of the road.

You can even make props that reflect their home and community lives. For example, place the furniture from a dollhouse near the blocks to invite children to represent their homes. With bits of fabric, children can create beds and talk about where they sleep, decorate tables and talk about how they eat, or wrap dolls and talk about how they dress up.

If the children are in a rural setting, laminate images of tractors and use binder clips to help the images stand up. For a city setting, make and attach neon signs with masking tape to tall block "skyscrapers." Or, instead of making some of these things for the children, invite the toddlers to work with you to explore how they might solve a problem—for example, you could place the tape near the block area and signs to give them an idea for attaching the signs.

Store back-up blocks nearby so that if a lot of toddlers are all excited about building the road at the same time, you can bring out more blocks fairly quickly. This is more effective than providing too many blocks all the time, which leads to clutter and invites dumping.

Expect to see toddlers using the blocks to build and invent, as props for dramatic play, and to investigate math and science concepts like comparing and balancing. Each class and each child is different; adapt this area to suit them. It's always an adventure to see what a group of children will choose to use the blocks for (Luckenbill & Shallock 2015)!

**Art and sensory area.** You can offer many open-ended activities at your art and sensory table. Consider materials for

> Sensory play: sand, potting soil with hidden objects, water, ice, bubble wrap
> Drawing, painting, sculpting, and other creations:
> natural clay, foamy paint, watercolor blocks
> Meaningful conversation: paint or paper that comes in a variety of skin tones
> Hand-eye coordination: scissors, stickers, tape, plastic eggs, glue bottles to squeeze (keep in mind that toddlers will completely empty glue bottles and finger paint with the glue!)
> Combining science with art: balls for rolling in a paint-filled box, paint to spin in a salad spinner

This is a great area for toddlers to engage in problem solving. Place several choices of materials on a low shelf—for example, stubby pencils, crayons, paper, and playdough—so children can express themselves, investigate the properties of the different materials, and take on interesting challenges.

How would you decide what to put on the art table or in sensory bins? Begin with what you see children doing, and put out open-ended, inviting items and materials that let them explore those interests and ideas further. Continue to use your observations to help you choose the materials and experiences you provide and the questions you ask children.

For example, you might notice that children were tracing their fingers in sand that spilled on the floor, which could lead you to place a thin layer of sand on trays with paste spreaders for making lines. Observing that children brought stacking cups to this area and used them to contain the sand might lead you to fill your sand and water bins with sand and cups of various sizes. You would comment on what you see the children doing, using the language of comparison to encourage math thinking: "It looks like you filled up a small cup and a big cup. I wonder if you are making a bigger pile."

Observing that the children were asking to add water to the sand to make it stick in castles, you might introduce water, which might lead you to phase out the regular sand in the water table but to extend the exploration of sand that sticks by bringing in magnetic sand.

If the children note that the magnetic sand is black, you might follow that lead, phasing out the magnetic sand and bringing in colorful sand the following week. This would allow you to sportscast color mixing and to compare the sand that sticks to magnet rods with colored sand that does not stick to the rods and to wonder why with the children.

Be careful not to take over too much when toddlers are investigating, particularly with art/science investigations. Children at this age are more focused on the doing than the results, and they are only beginning to grasp why something happens. The process of rolling or spinning is more important to them than understanding why or creating with a final product in mind.

**Cognitive (math/science/nature) area.** Here, focus on several general themes related to actions and cognitive strategies the toddlers are using: take apart, sort, connect, match, find patterns, categorize, problem solve, and use logic.

Don't address all the themes at once, but aim to get to each of them at some time in the year. It's okay for you to dwell on one concept for several weeks or to revisit these themes throughout the year. And it's okay to engage in several at a time in order to engage different children and their individual interests. Several concepts can be addressed with the same material—for example, a puzzle invites matching, problem solving, and spatial awareness.

Keeping key mathematical and scientific discoveries in mind, provide materials for a range of developmental levels. For example, include basic three-piece puzzles and some more complex ones with smaller knobs (nine pieces). This means that children with a range of fine motor skills can practice hand-eye coordination tasks at their own level.

To extend the concept of puzzles, provide a shape or volume challenge like a ball drop. To invite discoveries and problem solving with materials, intentionally provide balls that won't fit and collections of other items that might fit, so that some things will fit and some will not. With items for sorting near the ball drop, such as shells, stones, seeds, fruits, or plastic insects, toddlers are very likely to create their own investigations—they might put the nature items in the ball drops and discover new things about shape and how objects fit into different spaces.

Think about how you display your materials in this location to encourage particular types of discoveries. Put out objects for sorting, such as natural materials (pinecones), materials children use in their homes (bracelets), or plastic bears, and things to put them in, such as ice cube trays, muffin tins, or egg cartons. Placing the nature collections near the ball drop will invite children to test those materials in the toy. Placing baskets or clean egg cartons beside the nature collections mentioned above would invite grouping and counting.

Offer tools such as magnifying glasses for toddlers to test out on the nature collections and class pets (looking at pet frogs, for example), science toys such as magnets (bigger than choking size!), and large metal objects. Your goal is to bring things to toddlers' attention so they become interested in causation and begin to wonder with you about why things happen when you act on them (Schulz & Bonawitz 2007). Why do some things stick to the magnet rod and others don't, for example? You don't need to be an expert, and you don't need the answer—you just invite the toddlers to begin to think about the many interesting things that can happen.

It is not just causality that you are thinking about as toddlers begin to think in more complex ways. You can use sportscasting to make many math concepts visible in the cognitive area and other parts of the room and daily routine (Greenberg 2012). For example, Greenberg suggests these areas of focus for math talk with infants and toddlers: number and operations; shapes and spatial relationships; measurement; patterns, relationships, and change; and collecting and organizing information. Here are some simple ways you might draw these concepts to children's attention during play and other parts of the routine:

> **Number:** "I have three crackers and you have three crackers! Let's each eat one! Now we each have two! Do you want more?"

> **Measurement:** "You had a long nap today!" "That's a heavy pumpkin."

> **Patterns:** "You are wearing stripes! Red, blue, red, blue!" "Let's drum to the beat of the song together!"

> **Change:** "I think the beets in the garden grew bigger!" "Your diaper was wet—this one is dry."

> **Collecting and organizing information (like sorting):** "You put all the necklaces on your hand and all the bracelets on your wrist!" "You put the baby and the bottle together."

Look for opportunities to speak the language of math around children, using choices and questions that match their development. You might choose shells for the nature area with a range of colors, some bumpy, some smooth, some large, some small. These props invite the toddlers to observe attributes, but by sportscasting you can give them the language to talk about similarities and differences. You might also place containers near the shells to invite toddlers to group and sort them.

If toddlers are experimenting with dropping both the shells and the balls into the toy, you can talk about change: "The shells were up, but now they are down!" You can also help them notice patterns: "I see that the ball always fits, but the shells don't fit as easily. Sometimes you have to turn them around. I wonder why."

**Music area.** Continue to provide multiples of the same object in this area so toddlers can play alongside each other, imitating and learning from each other. For example, there might be three identical drums, each with two attached drumsticks. Add a little challenge to the area to invite problem solving, such as some drums without sticks and some rhythm sticks nearby. Include other items, such as pie pans, that invite toddlers to listen for and produce a range of sounds.

Bring math into your music area, too. Explore rhythm with tools like drums and shakers and differences in pitch with toys such as play pianos. Model patterns as you join in moving around this area with the children: "I'm going to go shake, shake, shake. Shake, shake, shake. Shake, shake, shake," Talk about what they're doing, "You played that one up high, and then you played it down low. That last note was in the middle."

Toddlers also play in this area through dance and movement. Model joyful dancing, inviting toddlers to join in with scarves, egg shakers, or instruments. This helps them refine their gross motor skills by making movements with their hands while their feet are doing something different. Start a parade to bring dramatic play to this area as well.

**Dramatic play area.** As toddlers' story lines become more complex, this area will probably take the most time and thought to design. To get ideas for materials and themes that are meaningful for the children, spend some time listening to them. Perhaps a toddler talks about her family's visit to the zoo, the group shares a collective passion for potties, or a family member shares that the family will go camping on the weekend.

Consider the children's home cultures. What kinds of activities do children experience that are unique to their families? How can you represent that in the dramatic play area? Medical experiences, for example, are common, and play around these experiences is very valuable for toddlers (see the vignette on page 84). Providing the opportunity to engage with real tools helps toddlers master their fears of them, and interacting with adults can help them determine what is real and what is imaginary, a line that toddlers struggle to find (Luckenbill & Zide 2017).

Once you have a real-life concept to explore, reflect on this group of toddlers' collective needs, including which elements should remain in the area from the current investigation because children are still interested in them. For example, if one toddler still uses medical play props to cope with a hospitalization, those props must remain available; you could shift them to another area or make them an element of the new design. Next, locate your materials and begin your design.

While dramatic play around what's familiar to toddlers is always important and popular, you can introduce children at this age to settings they have seen beyond the home. If you and the toddlers see a fire truck zoom past your classroom, you might design a social studies curriculum around firefighters. Provide props like firefighter costumes and boots, and tools such as lengths of hose and flashlights for toddlers to use to represent their ideas. You can even invite a firefighter to your classroom (or visit a station!) to extend the ideas around the play, asking that helper to talk about the things she wears and uses and why.

Based on that visit, you can further extend the curriculum. Transform your climber into a fire truck by adding short lengths of hose to the sides and a ladder on the back. Place the firefighter costumes on the climber or in baskets beside it and books about fire trucks on the shelves nearby. Display images in the area of firefighters from around the world (remember to include images of female firefighters) and the tools they use to fight fires.

You will find that the toddlers' firefighter play focuses primarily on getting into and out of the truck and "spraying" the hoses while wearing hats. This is more likely than a centralized goal of collectively fighting a fire or assigning roles for firefighting, because toddlers are generally focused on parallel play and are just beginning to pretend that an item like a climber can be used as a truck. Toddlers will need your support and scaffolding to engage in a play episode together.

Here are additional play themes toddlers might enjoy. Be sure you choose something they have some real-life experience with.

> Going to the doctor
> Moving
> Cleaning
> Going to a laundromat
> Shopping at a market or bodega
> Having a birthday party
> Gardening or working on a farm
> Having a pizza or going to a coffee or ice cream shop
> Going camping, fishing, picnicking, or to the beach
> Riding on a bus or train or flying in an airplane
> Hunting for treasure or going on a safari or zoo expedition (depending on the toddlers' life experiences and the community they live in)

**Outdoor play area.** When designing the outdoor space for your toddlers, feature the same interest topics as indoors when possible. Some areas need to be clearly defined, such as the block area, which needs a flat place for building, and the quiet area, which has soft materials that may need protection from rain. Other areas, like the art and sensory or nature and science areas, encompass the entire yard with its sand, soil, water, and plant life.

Outdoor experiences are more spontaneous, as you can rely to a degree on the season and what it brings to help you choose props. When you take time to ask "I wonder" questions to extend children's understanding of nature, you will find that teachable moments abound, and children are incredibly focused on the insect, puddle, or flower bush in question. Also, as you model interest in nature and science, comfort with nature and getting a bit dirty or muddy, and delight in big body play, you send a message to toddlers—nature is fascinating, and getting dirty and handling insects is part of exploring it!

## Designing the Play Space for Toddlers 30 to 36 Months

The design of room areas is much the same for older toddlers as it is for younger toddlers, with the same types of interest areas (see pages 92–106). Continue to provide items that invite them to investigate and problem solve, and provide open-ended ways for children to challenge themselves at their own levels.

**Design an area to value the child's idea.** When you design the dramatic play area for older toddlers, extending their play and learning might look like this: You have paid attention to a child's impulse to bake and to create a story line around cookies. With this in mind, you set up mixing bowls, whisks, silicone cupcake holders, and play ovens. Setting up an area to support a child's idea says to the child, "Yes, your idea is valued here." Changing the subject or ignoring the child's play cues sends a different message: "My adult idea is better than your idea."

**"Listen" to toddlers with your ears *and* eyes.** While toddlers generally are not yet ready to brainstorm ideas about props they might need for their play, they do tell us their ideas *with* their play. Careful observation tells you a lot about what children need.

For example, you might notice several conflicts occurring over the smaller plastic babies. Observing patterns of play, you note that these dolls are the only ones that fit in the plastic wheelchairs, another popular toy. These observations might lead you to expand medical play, adding more small dolls that fit in the wheelchairs and other exciting medical props to decrease the demand for the wheelchairs.

Observing toddler conversations is another way to gather data about curriculum. Here are a couple of examples.

Singing "Row, Row, Row Your Boat" at circle time, you might ask, "Oh, no, I see some sharks! Do you want to row slow or fast?" The idea of sharks is so exciting to one toddler that she later asks you to play being a shark. This leads to a play experience that includes a plastic bridge spanning two short staircases over a wading pool, with plastic sharks below.

This design lets children choose whether to lie down in the wading pool or hide from the sharks on the bridge above the pool. There is enough space for multiple children to play shark and even space for you to hide in the "water" and be the shark. There are also props—many soft and hard plastic fish, octopuses, and whales for children to sort, group, and use to represent the sea creatures in their games.

Here's another example: After you observe that toddlers love the song "Five Green and Speckled Frogs" and that they also enjoy leaping off stools, you create a frog pond by covering a queen-sized mattress with a blue sheet. You add real stumps around the pond for toddlers to jump from on to the mattress. Next to the mattress and stumps is a tree-shaped tunnel and puppet frogs, providing a quiet space for less active children to rest and hide. As the toddlers jump around in their "pond," you sing the song. In this way the toddlers control the curriculum with their idea and you expand on it, and the toddlers benefit as they explore the materials provided to extend their understanding of the song.

Let's sum up this strategy of observing children so you can provide experiences, materials, and interactions based on what you observe: Imagine yourself watching for clues about the toddlers' interests, asking yourself what props are needed to expand the learning, and then adapting by adding new materials or providing new social opportunities. After observing what happens with the initial provocation, imagine what you might do to adapt again, changing materials or adding more new props to extend the children's learning.

**Provide props that support diversity in building self-identities.** Older toddlers are just beginning to define themselves. They can often tell you about the things they like and don't like, their gender, what they observe about other people's differences, and other similar concepts. Providing a wide range of diverse props can help toddlers develop their understanding of their identities.

Family and societal attitudes may limit children's play. For example, a little boy may have been told not to use the pink dishes and kitchenette that belong to his sister at home and so may avoid the dramatic play area. In the classroom, it is important to let all children use all the props. This might look like boys trying on dresses and girls wearing construction hats. Avoid pink and blue playthings and instead use neutral-colored wood tones and realistic-looking kitchen items, particularly in the dramatic play area. Children will decide on their own how to define themselves, and limiting their access to materials can send a clear message about what you value about them and what you will not accept.

> Sarah at 33 Months
>
> Mama:  How does play make you feel?
> Sarah:  I dunno, happy?

## Adapting the Classroom Throughout the Year as Toddlers Grow

Toddler room lead teacher Lourdes Schallock shares insights about adapting her classroom throughout the year to her toddlers' changing interests and abilities (personal communication, March 2019):

> At the beginning of the year, when the toddlers are young, I plan the curriculum with their beginning abilities in mind. Some of the children still mouth everything, others have very basic fine motor skills, and others are still engaging in solitary play but interested in parallel play. When I set out materials and present provocations, I take into account their range of abilities to make sure they all have opportunities to be successful, and at the same time to make sure that they are all being challenged by the tasks they choose.
>
> As the year progresses, I change things to continue to challenge their growing abilities. (See the chart on the following page.)
>
> By the end of the year some of the children are practically preschoolers, so I set up the room according to their developmental needs and abilities, always keeping in mind the range of skills and developmental levels. There are always items set out with a specific child in mind. I can incorporate full themes by this time. One year we had a "going potty" theme with a semiprivate area with pretend potties and real toilet paper, trash cans, and pretend sinks and soap. We also had real underwear out for children to explore and some other clothing items to encourage them to put on a shirt, shoes, or hats, which many can do by the end of their time in the toddler room.

## Providing Challenges as Children's Abilities Grow

| Skill or area of development | Early in the program year | As the year progresses | By the end of the year |
|---|---|---|---|
| **Fine motor, cognitive** | Big knob puzzles<br><br>Finger crayons or block crayons<br><br>Basic three-hole shape sorter | Puzzles with smaller knobs that require pincer grasp<br><br>Chunky crayons<br><br>Pip-Squeaks markers (short and chunky but cylindrical) | Longer markers<br><br>Thinner colored pencils<br><br>Multisided shape sorter |
| **Building** | Soft blocks they can build with, knock down, and toss | Solid big blocks to stack and see how high they can go | A variety of wooden blocks, including smaller unit blocks to build roads, towers, or a zoo |
| **Books** | Simple picture books with a few words and very simple plots | Books that invite problem solving with flaps and questions | Books that contain more complex plots and characters |
| **Pretend and social play** | Several of the same item (at least three; more if the item is popular), such as basic shape sorters, dump trucks, cups, play foods, and cash registers for exploring parallel play | In dramatic play area, basic everyday items such as for pretend cooking (three of the same pot, three of the same spoon, and three of the same pretend foods)<br><br>As children begin to pretend to make pasta or other things they have experienced at home, provide additional items that relate to an emerging theme, such as making pasta, doing dishes, or making coffee | Items to extend the provocation based on children's interests and abilities, such as colanders for draining pasta or tongs for picking up the pipe cleaner pasta |

**Use your knowledge of child development and the children in your group to plan experiences that will enhance learning.** As we've emphasized throughout this book, observe children carefully and adapt the space and materials to support toddlers' emerging skills. You'll need both an understanding of developmental milestones and an awareness of each child's unique needs, especially if your program includes children with special needs. A developmental profile (such as the Desired Results Developmental Profile [California Department of Education 2015]) can help you understand what skills you might expect to come next based on what you see each child doing currently. Being aware of each toddler's emerging skills and understandings will help you know what kinds of materials to put out and the types of experiences each might enjoy and be ready for. See "Where to Find More" at the end of this chapter for other resources that can guide you as you develop developmentally appropriate program content.

These examples show ways teachers plan experiences that children can participate in wherever they are:

## Adapting play experiences to children's abilities

> Armand observes that the toddlers (24–30 months) in his classroom enjoy "catching fish," climbing, and hiding. All 12 children can mount stairs, but Isadora, having learned to walk at 24 months, is less steady in balancing than the others. Armand designs a "fishing" setup with two sets of stairs, one up and one down. In the center is a ladder, flat across

the steps and over the foam pond below. Since Isadora finds it challenging to climb a ladder by alternating her feet, there is a second "bridge"—the slide, also flat from one staircase to the other. All the children can crawl or walk across the easier challenge.

After observing that the toddlers in her group (26–30 months) can use each hand to do a different task (hand–eye coordination), and that many have been to the doctor recently, Catrina designs a medical office. Aware that some of the toddlers can quickly and easily open Band-Aids, while others cannot, she stays available to scaffold children through opening the Band-Aids. She encourages the entire group to do whichever parts they can on their own but steps in to help at different levels for each child. Over time Catrina invites all toddlers to try this on their own and adapts her assistance for each child based on her observations of their fine motor and hand-eye-coordination skills.

## Tinkering, Making, and Engineering with Toddlers

Tinkering is simply exploring open-ended materials—things to build with, connect, mix, mold, decorate with—and beginning to use tools (Heroman 2017). Making involves working toward an end product or creation. Both are child led and child designed, though you may help with the process. Engineering involves an adult-suggested problem to be solved, generating ideas, testing those ideas in practice, and revisiting the solution for possible refining and improvement (Heroman 2017).

As toddlers become young preschoolers, you will see that their creations become more intentional. Generally, they spend time tinkering with materials, then look at the thing they have made and label it. For example, they might roll out playdough into a snake shape and then tell you it is a snake rather than planning to make a snake and then rolling out the playdough. However, they are starting to think about their products being something and are likely to hand you "cookies," "tacos," and other named playdough delights.

When the toddlers become preschoolers, they will have a greater ability to reflect on abstract concepts, hold a plan or idea in mind, and problem solve around that idea, so you are more likely to see engineering after the children have left your classroom.

This said, you can invite older toddlers to use basic elements of engineering. Toddler lead teacher Lourdes Schallock has done a great deal of research into engineering with toddlers and notes that "toddlers engage in the engineering process anytime they interact with their environment. As a teacher I facilitate their experience by giving them the language and support they need in their explorations and as they engage in the different steps of the engineering process." She offers the following steps and strategies (personal communication, March 2019).

**1** **Step one: Acknowledge their question or problem.** What is the problem or objective; what is the child trying to do? There are different ways to acknowledge this, depending on the child and the activity. You might say, "I see the ball got stuck in the tube and you are trying to get it out," or "The stack is wobbly—are you trying to put one more block on top?," or "The car isn't rolling up the ramp when you push it."

**2** **Step two: Encourage children to imagine possible solutions** and act on them. Some toddlers will respond or talk about what they are doing, but most will move from step to step without much communication. As you quietly observe how they approach the problem, ask "I wonder" questions to suggest ideas. For example, try "I wonder if you want to move or tilt the tube," or "I wonder how you can make the tower more stable so it won't keep falling when you put the last block on it," or "You are pushing the car very gently. I wonder what happens if you push it harder." This allows them the freedom to take your ideas or leave them. Your goal is to facilitate the process. As frustrating as it may be to watch, let them lead, and don't give them the answer. Pave the way to a successful outcome, even if it is not one that makes adult sense.

**3** **Step three: Create or build.** As toddlers act on their solution plan, they will probably need materials to do so. Provide plenty of room to work. Strategically set out materials they might need or suggest possibilities, and be vigilant so that other children do not take their materials.

Scaffold and support their solution approach by narrating their actions. For example: "You are lifting the tube a little bit, I can hear the ball rolling slowly in there, but it's not coming out! . . . I wonder what happens if you make it roll faster. How can you do that? . . . Oh, you lifted the tube higher . . . the ball came out!"

**4** **Step four: Adjust their ideas.** As children try different ways of solving their problem, continue to support them until they accomplish their goal. Some toddlers might give up; help them persevere by narrating what they are doing, what worked, what didn't, and why. For example: "You almost made the car roll up the ramp. Try again. I wonder if you can push it harder this time. . . . Oh, you pushed harder, and it went higher! One more time—you can do it! . . . Oh, you did it! You pushed much harder and the car rolled all the way up the ramp. You used a lot of force!" As you narrate, carefully choose your words, keeping the language simple, rich, and accurate.

Toddlers may enter the engineering process at any step or go back and forth between just two of the steps. Most toddlers start by creating something or trying to accomplish a task first, and then encounter a problem to solve. Your goal is to support and encourage them and suggest ideas without taking over the project. Some toddlers will engage for a long time, and others will quickly go off to explore other areas. And that's okay.

Joining toddlers in play is an adventure. They think so differently from their teachers that you never know what will happen! Toddlers are constantly testing the limits of their world—what their bodies, their toys and materials, and their coplayers will do—and the results can be both challenging and humorous. As a toddler teacher, you use every tool in your toolkit, being persistent, engaged, quick to respond, and funny, and when you do, you will be surprised and delighted by where you and the toddlers will go.

# Where to Find More:
## Resources for Teachers and Families

"BRAULT Behavior Checklist": www.braultbehavior.org/uploads/1/6/9/8/16982342/braultbehaviorchecklist.pdf

*Children with Challenging Behaviors: Strategies for Reflective Thinking,* by L. Brault and T. Brault (CPG Publishing, 2005)

*A High-Quality Program for Your Toddler* (NAEYC, 2017)

"I Want It My Way: Problem-Solving Techniques with Children Two to Eight," by S. Dinwiddie: http://webshare.northseattle.edu/fam180/topics/communication/IWantItMyWay.htm

*Making and Tinkering With STEM: Solving Design Challenges With Young Children*, by C. Heroman (NAEYC, 2017)

"STEM Moments: Everyday Fun with Engineering and Technology": http://talkingisteaching.org/assets/general/Everyday-Fun-With-Engineering.pdf

"Tips for Choosing Toys for Toddlers," by R. Parlakian: www.zerotothree.org/resources/1076-tips-for-choosing-toys-for-toddlers

*The What, Why, and How of High-Quality Programs for Toddlers: The Guide for Families* (NAEYC, 2016)

# 5

# Working with Children with Diverse Characteristics, Abilities, and Needs

You're likely to have children with a range of abilities and needs in your group, including infants and toddlers with a delay or disability. Wherever children are in their development, you can adapt the space, curriculum, and your own interactions to support them.

It may seem intimidating to design a classroom that is inclusive of all children, but you *can* create comfortable places for infants and toddlers from all backgrounds and with all levels of ability to learn and grow. While factors like having well-qualified staff and small group sizes and ratios are important, you may face less than ideal conditions in your program. You can still focus on providing a positive and healthy learning environment, designing curriculum that is developmentally appropriate for all the children, and treating families as partners. Throughout this book, you've seen a number of ways to offer different levels of complexity in the experiences you present. Additional suggestions are presented in this chapter.

Keep in mind that play is the work of all children, so wherever a child is developmentally, the space must be accessible for play, tailored to the child's interests and abilities, and safe for exploring in open-ended ways. This may mean that you change your room design so items can be reached from a lower space (on the floor) or higher (from a wheelchair). You may need to adapt materials to help children be successful, like using self-adhesive medical wrap to make the handles of a rolling pin easier to grasp. Be sure children can reach and use the materials and make choices—this is key for supporting children as they explore cause and effect, problem solve, and engage in creative play.

You may also need to consider other elements to set children up for successful play. It's challenging for a child who is hard of hearing to pick up on play cues and hear your sportscasting when there is a lot of background noise. Consider limiting music in the background when not offering a dance activity or doing music activities outside. If a child is easily overwhelmed by sensory experiences, be sure to offer tools to facilitate exploration—he may feel comfortable using a stick to poke the foam paint if he does not want to touch it directly.

# Partner with Families Using a Strengths-Based Model

Many families compare their children to the other children they observe in the community. Outside the classroom, it's common to hear about how high each child can count, how toilet trained each child is, how beautifully they sleep through the night, and how clever they are at solving puzzles.

For family members of children with delays, these conversations may be painful. It's important to help these family members find support, not just through their child's therapists and doctors but also from other families who have experienced similar situations. Knowing that their child will continue to grow and develop skills, though at his own pace and in a unique way, is important to hear.

To get a better picture of a child's play capabilities in a range of situations, invite families to be observational partners with you. Since families are experts on their own child and have often done their own research or sought out specialists for guidance, their viewpoint is valuable to the ongoing process of including their child in the classroom. This said, families look to you as the expert in your classroom's culture, expectations, and routines, and they need you to identify ways their child can grow in your space.

As you include children with disabilities, you must consider how to best support the child's play and interactions with the other children in your classroom. You may find that some families of children with disabilities are not ready for their child to take on classroom challenges that you think are appropriate. Consider that families may have a strong inclination to protect their children from taking physical risks or moving out of their comfort zones. By documenting what a child is doing in your setting, through photography and video, you can share the child's strengths with her family in ongoing conferences, then talk about building on those strengths to encourage development by inviting the child to take small risks or move a bit out of her comfort zone.

Starting with capabilities before talking about things to work on sets the stage for families to see children as capable learners, individuals who are always growing and moving forward, at their own pace. As they see their child's successes at school, parents are often eager are to join you in creating similar experiences at home, as Layla's parents are:

> Teacher: Look, see how Layla can sit up in her chair? She's much stronger than just a month or so ago. We'll try offering art at a little table rather than in her high chair.
> Parent: I didn't know she could do that! We can try that too.

# Strategies for Supporting Children in Play

Many children with delays or disabilities may need simple modifications to activities or materials, and others will need more support. As you consider how to help all the children be successful in play, look at your environment, routines, and the ways you interact with children and how they relate to each other. It starts with seeing children as children first and remembering that best practices are best practices for *all* children.

For example, including a child with hearing loss means avoiding playing music in the background of the classroom except when it is planned for dancing or a similar activity. But creating a communication-friendly space where teachers and children can hear each other and where music playing is intentional is best practice for all children as they expand their language skills.

## Use a Child-Centered Approach to Shift from a Disability Mindset

Using a child-centered approach, you view the child as a child first and as a child who has a delay or disability second. So instead of including "a Down syndrome child" in your program, you include Melissa, who has Down syndrome. Then you can examine the many ways that Melissa can play across the developmental domains. This helps you focus on what a child can do and leads to discoveries: That she is very capable, even surpassing other children her age in some activities, such as showing empathy during peer interactions or connecting with you in games like peekaboo. In other play activities she may need more support, such as dressing up, climbing, and/or verbal communication so her peers can understand what she wants to play. As you join her in play and work hand in hand with her family and her therapists on ways to support her, you'll observe her growing skills and confidence and celebrate her competencies.

### Including a toddler with developmental delays

Zenobia joined the toddler room when she was 24 months old. She had had a major birth trauma and exhibited developmental delays in language and gross motor skills. Including Zenobia in the classroom meant working closely both with her family and her occupational therapist to provide appropriate play experiences. Zenobia was able to join her peers in activities such as art. She loved playdough and water play, and participating in these activities gave her a space where she could join in parallel play with the other children.

Teachers Hannah and Shelby adapted gross motor experiences such as climbing by staying close to Zenobia and coaching her. They also provided alternative ways she could be successful, like using the simpler stairs to get up the climber while peers used the more complex rock wall. All of the toddlers in the room used both gestures and speech to communicate, so Zenobia's language delay was easily accommodated, and she could use a gesture or words to join peers in play. Hannah and Shelby observed that Zenobia was a valued member of the toddler community rather than excluded for her differences, and that she was often invited into play with the other children. One memorable day, she raced down from the loft while several other toddlers stood at the bottom, waving flags and cheering for her.

# Adapt Experiences to Meet Children's Unique Needs

While a child's interests and abilities may differ from those of her peers, you can adapt experiences to be age appropriate while supporting the child's interests (perhaps in shaking, mouthing, and banging things). This will allow her to join in with her age mates in the same activities. For example, if all the children enjoy shaking to music, add shaker eggs to make this an inclusive experience for a child who is in the toddler room and whose interests are developmentally more suited to the infant room.

You may have infants or toddlers in your room who do not have a disability but need your focused support for other reasons. A child with a background of abuse or neglect or who has undergone extensive hospitalization may not initially seek you out for play or feel comfortable playing in the classroom. For this child, you may need to design special time in or focused one-on-one play and coaching to help her learn that the classroom is a place where she can trust and feel safe.

For dual language learners, communicating in their home languages is key to their comfort and success in the classroom. In Xiao Ming's case, there were student teachers in the program who spoke his language:

### Supporting a dual language learner

Xiao Ming joined the toddler room when he was 25 months old. He spoke only Mandarin and until recently lived in China with his grandparents. At first he was too afraid to play, but his patient Mandarin-speaking student teachers discovered his passion for airplanes, art, and nature and designed play experiences for him. They put plastic airplanes on the shelf, included water play in the garden, and joined him in harvesting celery and tasting it. These moments of shared focus on his play and interests led to longer periods of relaxed play in the block area and yard, and over time he was able to engage his peers in activities such as bubble blowing and digging a group hole, even using a few words of English with them. Key to his success were the teachers willing to use words in his home language.

Your program may not have a staff member or student who speaks a child's home language. Work with families and community partners to find someone who can, and learn some words in the language yourself, even if just a few.

# Facilitate Play with Other Children

Children with disabilities sometimes struggle to enter play with their peers. This can be due to a physical barrier such as being unable to hear play cues, a physical challenge like struggling to keep up with other toddlers pushing carts quickly on the bike path, or social challenges like finding it uncomfortable to make eye contact or be in close physical interactions with others. You must be a play coach for children, becoming the bridge for connection and offering tips for interaction. For example, you might stay close by to point out social cues to a child and his peers:

"Look, Rashid, Oliver is smiling at you. I think he likes when you play chase. I bet he'd like to do it again."

Look for ways to include all children in your classroom culture. Encourage everyone to learn a few signs to use with a child with hearing loss. Design the classroom to invite exploration in different ways and at multiple levels.

## Customize Your Toolkit to Each Child

You'll try out many new tools to help all children as they develop play skills, supporting each one as he becomes increasingly capable. Each child who joins your community is unique, deserving of an individualized, responsive approach. You have an important role to play as you adapt to each one's needs and create an individualized yet communal space to grow, play, and learn.

How do you do this?

> **Use quality assessments to help design experiences.** You begin by paying close attention, observing and documenting a child's activities, emotions, interactions, abilities, and achievements. You can use a high-quality child assessment tool designed for use with infants and toddlers, such as California's Desired Results Developmental Profile (DRDP), or tools designed to work with widely used curriculum frameworks for infants and toddlers, such as the Creative Curriculum GOLD assessment system or HighScope's COR Advantage. This helps to keep your documentation broad based, objective, and based on a child's own play activities in the care and education setting. Once you have gathered the information you need and considered which skills might be emerging next, you can design experiences to support those skills, using the strategies discussed in previous chapters.

> **Apply your personal experience and knowledge of child development.** It is important to recognize that your expertise lies in the knowledge of child development and your ability to observe, reflect, and adapt as you actively engage with children in their daily activities and support new skills through your curriculum and interactions. While evaluation, diagnosis, appropriate labeling of developmental differences, and specific therapeutic strategies are the job of medical and early intervention specialists—and it's vital to work closely with them where possible—trust your own instincts and expertise in supporting the learning and development of all infants and toddlers.

### Including a child with medical needs in the infant room

LeShawn and his family joined the infant room when he was 11 months old. LeShawn's gastrointestinal condition was diagnosed at birth, and he spent his early life in the hospital undergoing multiple painful procedures and nearly died. Including LeShawn in the program meant learning about his G-tube and specialized feeding needs and how to handle his deep (and realistic) distrust of nonfamily. (Most strangers in the hospital smile while causing pain, a confusing message for infants who are learning to trust others).

The teachers found that including an 11-month-old in the program with the motor and feeding skills of a 3-month-old but the cognitive skills typical of his age was not a challenge. They already served nonmobile infants who needed staff to assist in feeding, and they could bring age-appropriate curriculum items to LeShawn's side and join him as he explored them. Designing curriculum for LeShawn included adding medical play props to the classroom so he could act out his very real fears and through play master his feelings about real medical tools. The teachers were also aware that he was very sensitive to touch, as he would often get distraught when peers brushed or bumped him during play. With coaching, the other toddlers began to notice his tears and would help calm him, bringing his family's photograph or singing to him. The empathy he helped everyone develop, families and children alike, was a gift.

---

Including children with diverse abilities in your classroom community is a gift for everyone. You will find yourself stretching and growing, trying new ways of doing things and adding new skills to your teaching toolkit as you help children join in the play in meaningful ways. Working with specialists in a child's disability may even teach you new ways to engage the child's peers and support children who do not qualify for special services. Though inclusion does often involve extra work, both in documenting learning and in designing curriculum, the reward of seeing every child thrive and grow, taking on new play challenges every day, makes the process incredibly worthwhile.

# Where to Find More:
## Resources for Teachers and Families

"Adapting the Child Care Environment for Children with Special Needs": https://articles.extension.org/pages/61358/adapting-the-child-care-environment-for-children-with-special-needs

"The Daily Dozen: Strategies for Enhancing Social Communication of Infants with Language Delays," by N. Stockall and L.R. Dennis (*Young Children*, Vol. 67, No. 4, pp. 36–41, September 2012)

"Enhancing Practice with Infants and Toddlers from Diverse Language and Cultural Backgrounds," by K. Nemeth and V. Erdosi (*Young Children*, Vol. 67, No. 4, pp. 49–57, September 2012)

"Inclusion in Infant/Toddler Child Development Settings: More than Just Including," by R. Parlakian (*Young Children*, Vol. 67, No. 4, pp. 49–57, September 2012)

"Supporting Medical Fragile Children and Their Families," by J. Luckenbill and A. Zide (*Young Children*, Vol. 72, No. 4, pp. 79–84, September 2017): NAEYC.org/resources/pubs/yc/sep2017/supporting-medically-fragile-children

# Conclusion

As infants and toddlers explore their world through play, your role as teacher is central. You observe, engage, and create. You observe in order to learn as much as you can about each child's interests, abilities, and developmental progress. You engage in order to be a responsive play partner and a facilitator of new skills and understanding. You create as you document, reflect on your shared experiences with the children, and continue to develop environments and curriculum that will challenge young children to learn.

When you are a teacher of infants and toddlers, every day is eventful and may seem hectic. Much of your activity is built around routines, and in fact may often come to seem too routine—centered predictably around feeding, dressing, comforting, and cleaning up. But every one of those routines can be accomplished playfully in ways that strengthen your bonds with children through your shared experiences. "Where's your sock? There it is!" can be repeated day after day and still elicit smiles from both teacher and child. Maintaining your sense of humor and perspective about the small stuff can lighten the burden and help set a positive tone for whatever comes. And creating a song or ritual prompted by a child's new skill or discovery shows him that you notice and value his efforts and interests. Showing your pleasure and voicing your thoughts reminds a toddler that you are a very real person who is also a playful, engaged partner.

This essential interplay of young child and teacher is captured in Donald Winnicott's famous line, "There is no such thing as a baby . . . you are describing a baby and someone" (1957, 137). Very young children become competent and confident as you build the warm, caring relationships they need. When you are their secure base in the classroom, you let each child know they can trust you to support their independent efforts. As you celebrate their delighted discoveries with joy, your shared adventures will nurture both of you.

## Acknowledgments

We are grateful to the CCFS families, children, and teachers whose stories fill this book, and to our families for their support and patience. A special thank-you goes to Deedee Levine and Ross Thompson, who assisted with both research and editing of the book.

# References

Balaban, N. 2011. "Easing the Separation Process for Infants, Toddlers, and Families." In *Spotlight on Infants and Toddlers,* eds. D. Koralek & L.G. Gillespie, 14–20. Washington, DC: NAEYC.

Berk, L., & A. Meyers. 2013. "The Role of Make-Believe Play in the Development of Executive Function: Status of Research and Future Directions." *American Journal of Play* 6 (1): 98–110.

Bonawitz, E.L., P. Shafto, H. Gweon, N.D. Goodman, E. Spelke, & L. Schulz. 2011. "The Double-Edged Sword of Pedagogy: Instruction Limits Spontaneous Exploration and Discovery." *Cognition* 120 (3): 322–30. doi:10.1016/j.cognition.2010.10.001.

Bongiorno, L. 2019. "Play and Learning Go Hand in Hand." In *Serious Fun: How Guided Play Extends Children's Learning,* eds. M.L. Masterson & H. Bohart, 116–117. Washington, DC: NAEYC.

Bornstein, M.H., M.E. Arterberry, & M.E. Lamb. 2013. *Development in Infancy: A Contemporary Introduction.* 5th ed. New York: Psychology Press.

California Department of Education. 2015. *DRDP: A Developmental Continuum from Early Infancy to Kindergarten Entry. Infant and Toddler View.* Sacramento: California Department of Education. www.cde.ca.gov/sp/Cd/ci/documents/drdp2015infanttoddler.pdf.

Carlson, F.M. 2011. *Big Body Play: Why Boisterous, Vigorous, and Very Physical Play Is Essential to Children's Development and Learning.* Washington, DC: NAEYC.

Cohen, L.E., & J. Emmons. 2017. "Block Play: Spatial Language with Preschool and School-Aged Children." *Early Child Development and Care* 187 (5/6): 967–77.

Csikszentmihalyi, M. 2014. *Flow and the Foundations of Positive Psychology: The Collected Works of Mihaly Csikszentmihalyi.* Vol. 2. New York: Springer.

Da Ros, D.A., & B.A. Kovach. 1998. "Assisting Toddlers and Caregivers During Conflict Resolutions: Interactions that Promote Socialization." *Childhood Education* 75 (1): 25–30.

Elkind, D. 2008. "The Power of Play: Learning What Comes Naturally." *American Journal of Play* 1 (1): 1–6. www.journalofplay.org/sites/www.journalofplay.org/files/pdf-articles/1-1-article-elkind-the-power-of-play.pdf.

Erikson, E.H. 1950. *Childhood and Society.* New York: Norton.

Erikson Institute Early Math Collaborative. n.d. "Precursor Concepts." Accessed January 1, 2017. https://earlymath.erikson.edu/why-early-math-everyday-math/precursor-concepts.

Evans, B. 2016. *You Can't Come to My Birthday Party! Conflict Resolution with Young Children.* 2nd ed. Ypsilanti, MI: HighScope Press.

Galinsky, E. 2010. *Mind in the Making: The Seven Essential Life Skills Every Child Needs.* New York: Harper Collins.

Gerber, R.J., T. Wilks, & C. Erdie-Lalena. 2010. "Developmental Milestones: Motor Development." *Pediatrics in Review* 31 (7): 267–76. https://pedsinreview.aappublications.org/content/pedsinreview/31/7/267.full.pdf.

Gillespie, L.G., & J.D. Greenberg. 2017. "Empowering Infants' and Toddlers' Learning Through Scaffolding." Rocking and Rolling. *Young Children* 72 (2): 90–93. www.naeyc.org/resources/pubs/yc/may2017/rocking-and-rolling-empowering-infants-and-toddlers.

Gopnik, A. 2009. *The Philosophical Baby: What Children's Minds Tell Us About Truth, Love, and the Meaning of Life.* New York: Farrar, Straus and Giroux.

Gray, P. 2008. "The Value of Play I: The Definition of Play Gives Insights." *Psychology Today: Freedom to Learn* (blog). November 19. www.psychologytoday.com/blog/freedom -learn/200811/the-value-play-i-the-definition -play-gives-insights.

Greenberg, J. 2012. "More, All Gone, Empty, Full: Math Talk Every Day in Every Way." *Young Children* 67 (3): 62–64.

Greenspan, S. 2011. "Emotional Development in Infants and Toddlers." In *Infant/Toddler Caregiving: A Guide to Social-Emotional Growth and Socialization,* 2nd ed., ed. J.R. Lally, 15–18. Sacramento: California Department of Education. www.cde.ca.gov/sp /cd/re/documents/pitcguidesocemo2011.pdf.

Greenspan, S. With N.B. Lewis. 1999. *Building Healthy Minds: The Six Experiences That Create Intelligence and Emotional Growth in Babies and Young Children*. New York: Da Capo.

Gross, D. 2008. *Infancy: Development from Birth to Age 3*. Boston: Allyn & Bacon.

Halle, T., R. Anderson, A. Blasberg, A. Chrisler, & S. Simkin. 2011. *Quality of Caregiver-Child Interactions for Infants and Toddlers (Q-CCIIT). A Review of the Literature.* Washington, DC: Office of Planning, Research, and Evaluation, Administration for Children and Families, US Department of Health and Human Services.

Heroman, C. 2017. *Making and Tinkering With STEM: Solving Design Challenges With Young Children*. Washington, DC: NAEYC.

Karp, H. 2015. *The Happiest Baby on The Block: The New Way to Calm Crying and Help Your Newborn Baby Sleep Longer*. 2nd ed. New York: Bantam Books.

Kid Sense. n.d. "Play and Social Skills." Accessed April 25, 2019. https://childdevelopment .au/areas-of-concern/play-and-social-skills.

Kirk, E., N. Howlett, K.J. Pine, & B.C. Fletcher. 2012. "To Sign or Not to Sign? The Impact of Encouraging Infants to Gesture on Infant Language and Maternal Mind-Mindedness." *Child Development* 84 (2): 574–90.

Lally, J.R., P.L. Mangione, S. Signer, & G.O. Butterfield. 1998. *Early Messages: Facilitating Language Development and Communication.* DVD. Sacramento: California Department of Education.

Lally, J.R., P.L. Mangione, S. Signer, G.O. Butterfield, & S. Gilford. 1990. *Getting in Tune: Creating Nurturing Relationships with Infants and Toddlers*. The Program for Infant/ Toddler Caregivers (developed collaboratively by the California Department of Education and WestEd). www.pitc.org/cs/pitclib/view /pitc_res/816.

Lally, J.R., J. Stewart, & D. Greenwald, eds. 2009. *Infant/Toddler Caregiving: A Guide to Setting Up Environments*. 2nd ed. Sacramento: California Department of Education.

Luckenbill J. 2012. "Getting the Picture: Using the Digital Camera as a Tool to Support Reflective Practice and Responsive Care." *Young Children* 67 (2): 28–36.

Luckenbill, J., & L. Shallock. 2015. "Designing and Using a Developmentally Appropriate Block Area for Infants and Toddlers." *Young Children* 70 (1): 8–17.

Luckenbill, J., & A. Zide. 2017. "Supporting Medically Fragile Children and Their Families." *Young Children* 72 (4): 79–84. www.naeyc .org/resources/pubs/yc/sep2017/supporting -medically-fragile-children.

Maguire-Fong, M.J. 2015. *Teaching and Learning with Infants and Toddlers: Where Meaning Making Begins*. San Francisco: WestEd.

Mahler, M.S., F. Pine, & A. Bergman. 1975. *The Psychological Birth of the Human Infant: Symbiosis and Individuation*. London: Hutchinson & Co.

NAEYC. 2009. "Developmentally Appropriate Practice in Early Childhood Programs Serving Children Birth through Age 8." Position statement. Washington, DC: NAEYC. www.naeyc.org/sites/default/files/globally-shared/downloads/PDFs/resources/position-statements/PSDAP.pdf.

Pathways.org. 2019. *Play: It's More than You Think.* Brochure. https://pathways.org/wp-content/uploads/2016/03/PlayBrochure_LEGAL.pdf.

Petersen, S. 2012. "School Readiness for Infants and Toddlers? Really? Yes, Really!" *Young Children* 67 (4): 10–13.

Ramani, G.B. 2012. "Influence of a Playful, Child-Directed Context on Preschool Children's Peer Cooperation." *Merrill-Palmer Quarterly* 58 (2): 159–90.

Schulz, L.E., & E.B. Bonawitz. 2007. "Serious Fun: Preschoolers Engage in More Exploratory Play When Evidence Is Confounded." *Developmental Psychology* 43 (4): 1045–50.

Schwarz, T., & J. Luckenbill. 2012. "Let's Get Messy! Exploring Sensory and Art Activities with Infants and Toddlers." *Young Children* 67 (4): 26–35.

Shumaker, H. 2012. *It's OK Not to Share . . . And Other Renegade Rules for Raising Competent and Compassionate Kids.* New York: Jeremy P. Tarcher/Penguin.

Stahl, A.E., & L. Feigenson. 2015. "Observing the Unexpected Enhances Infants' Learning and Exploration." *Science* 348 (6230): 91–4.

Stifter, C.A., & D. Moyer. 1991. "The Regulation of Positive Affect: Gaze Aversion Activity During Mother-Infant Interaction." *Infant Behavior and Development* 14 (1): 111–23.

Vaish, A., M. Carpenter, & M. Tomasello. 2016. "The Early Emergence of Guilt-Motivated Prosocial Behavior." *Child Development* 87 (6): 1772–82. doi:10.1111/cdev.12628.

Wanerman, T. 2015. "Engage-Reflect-Plan: An Introduction to Inclusive Support of Diverse Learners." Teacher in-service presentation, Gan Haverim Preschool, Davis, CA, August 25.

Wang, J., & K.C. Barrett. 2013. "Mastery Motivation and Self-Regulation During Early Childhood." In *Handbook of Self-Regulatory Processes in Development: New Directions and International Perspectives,* eds. K.C. Barrett, N.A. Fox, G.A. Morgan, D.J. Fidler, & L.A. Daunhauer, 337–80. New York: Psychology Press.

Waters, S.F., T.V. West, & W.B. Mendes. 2014. "Stress Contagion: Physiological Covariation Between Mothers and Infants." *Psychological Science* 25 (4): 934–42.

White, R.E. n.d. *The Power of Play: A Research Summary on Play and Learning.* St. Paul: Minnesota Children's Museum. Accessed April 26, 2019. www.childrensmuseums.org/images/MCMResearchSummary.pdf.

Williamson, G.G., & M.E. Anzalone. 2001. *Sensory Integration and Self-Regulation in Infants and Toddlers: Helping Very Young Children Interact with Their Environment.* Washington, DC: ZERO TO THREE.

Winnicott, D.W. 1957. "Further Thoughts on Babies as Persons." In *The Child and the Outside World: Studies in Developing Relationships,* ed. J. Hardenberg, 134–40. London: Tavistock. First published 1947.

Yogman, M., A. Garner, J. Hutchinson, K. Hirsh-Pasek, & R.M. Golinkoff. 2018. *The Power of Play: A Pediatric Role in Enhancing Development in Young Children.* Report of the AAP Committee on Psychosocial Aspects of Child and Family Health, AA Council on Communications and Media. *Pediatrics* 142 (3): e20182058.

ZERO TO THREE. 2016. "Developing Thinking Skills From 24–36 Months." May 19. www.zerotothree.org/resources/1290-developing-thinking-skills-from-24-36-months.

This Is Play

# About the Authors

**Julia Luckenbill,** MA, is the program coordinator for the infant–toddler program at the NAEYC-accredited Early Childhood Laboratory School (ECL) at the University of California, Davis (UC Davis), Center for Child and Family Studies (CCFS). She is also a child development demonstration lecturer. A frequent contributor to NAEYC's periodicals and blogs, she presents at NAEYC conferences and elsewhere on child development topics for families, teachers, and students.

Julia's many interests including using puppetry to teach social and emotional skills, integrating LGBTQI families in early childhood settings, using photography to document children's learning and coach adults, making farm-to-school connections, and integrating medically fragile children and child life practices in early childhood education settings. She lives with her partner and kindergartner and enjoys painting rocks in her spare time.

**Aarti Subramaniam,** PhD, is a research analyst for the University of California Agriculture and Natural Resources 4-H youth development program. Her work has supported youth development professionals and practitioners working with children and adolescents in learning programs that include garden-based learning, camp programs, environmental science, and youth leadership. Her areas of interest include learning environments that are empowering for children and young people, authentic assessment, and learning outside the classroom. She has authored articles in journals such as *Journal of Youth Development* and *Children, Youth and Environments.*

**Janet Thompson,** MA, is director of the Early Childhood Lab (ECL) School at the UC, Davis, CCFS. She has established the school's outdoor spaces as a Certified Nature Explore Classroom and works with families, teachers, and college students on ways to design and use outdoor environments to enhance children's learning and health. She has a particular interest in social and emotional competency and its contributions to early learning and is a strong advocate for active learning approaches that emphasize responsive adult–child interactions.

Janet was a primary author on social-emotional development for the California Department of Education's *Preschool Learning Foundations* and *Preschool Curriculum Frameworks* and a contributing author for the *California Preschool Program Guidelines.*

# Discover NAEYC!

The National Association for the Education of Young Children (NAEYC) promotes high-quality early learning for all young children, birth through age 8, by connecting early childhood practice, policy, and research. We advance a diverse, dynamic early childhood profession and support all who care for, educate, and work on behalf of young children.

NAEYC members have access to award-winning publications, professional development, networking opportunities, professional liability insurance, and an array of members-only discounts.

## Accreditation—NAEYC.org/accreditation

Across the country, **NAEYC Accreditation of Early Learning Programs** and **NAEYC Accreditation of Early Childhood Higher Education Programs** set the industry standards for quality in early childhood education. These systems use research-based standards to recognize excellence in the field of early childhood education.

## Advocacy and Public Policy—NAEYC.org/policy

NAEYC is a leader in promoting and advocating for policies at the local, state, and federal levels that expand opportunities for all children to have equitable access to high-quality early learning. NAEYC is also dedicated to promoting policies that value early childhood educators and support their excellence.

## Global Engagement—NAEYC.org/global

NAEYC's Global Engagement department works with governments and other large-scale systems to create guidelines to support early learning, as well as early childhood professionals throughout the world.

## Professional Learning—NAEYC.org/ecp

NAEYC provides face-to-face training, technology-based learning, and Accreditation workshops—all leading to improvements in the knowledge, skills, and practices of early childhood professionals.

## Publications and Resources—NAEYC.org/publications

NAEYC publishes some of the most valued resources for early childhood professionals, including award-winning books, *Teaching Young Children* magazine, and *Young Children*, the association's peer-reviewed journal. NAEYC publications focus on developmentally appropriate practice and enable members to stay up to date on current research and emerging trends, with information they can apply directly to their classroom practice.

## Signature Events—NAEYC.org/events

NAEYC hosts three of the most important and well-attended annual events for educators, students, administrators, and advocates in the early learning community.

**NAEYC's Annual Conference** is the world's largest gathering of early childhood professionals.

**NAEYC's Professional Learning Institute** is the premier professional development conference for early childhood trainers, faculty members, researchers, systems administrators, and other professionals.

The **NAEYC Public Policy Forum** provides members with resources, training, and networking opportunities to build advocacy skills and relationships with policymakers on Capitol Hill.